FASHION
COMPUTING

Design techniques
and CAD

SANDRA BURKE

www.burkepublishing.com   www.fashionbooks.info

Fashion Computing - *Design Techniques and CAD*
Sandra Burke

ISBN - 13: 9-780958-239134
ISBN - 10: 0-9582391-3-4

Reprint: 2007
Published: 2006

Copyright ©:   Burke Publishing
                    Email: sandra@burkepublishing.com
                    Website: www.burkepublishing.com (Instructor's Manual)
                    Website: www.fashionbooks.info

Distributors: **UK:** Marston Book Services Limited, email: trade.enq@marston.co.uk
                    USA: Partners Book Distributing, email: partnersbk@aol.com
                    South Africa: Blue Weaver Marketing, email: orders@blueweaver.co.za
                    Australia: Thames and Hudson, email: orders@thaust.com.au
                    Hong Kong: Publishers Associates Ltd (PAL), email: pal@netvigator.com

DTP: Sandra Burke
Cover Design: Sophia Spivak and Simon Larkin
Printed: Everbest Printers, China

Text Notes: The exercises described in *Fashion Computing* may vary depending on the version of software you are using. While these are 'basic' exercises and might not change with later versions, the reader should be aware that software development does not stand still and changes in techniques may be required in future versions.
UK and US dictionaries have been used where appropriate.

ISBN - 13: 9-780958-239134
ISBN - 10: 0-9582391-3-4

 **Dedication........**to Linda, Oliver and Sophie, dedicated followers of fashion, from catwalk to street, fashion shoot to pavement.......jetting off to every corner of the fashion world, from Cape Town to London, and New York to Hong Kong, searching out the latest trends.

Fashion shoot: Make-up, lights, camera! Esther being made up for the fashion shoot by hair and make-up artist Miranda Raman. Photographer, Louise Davies.

content

1 **getting started - 10**

intro - 11, history - 11, the aim of this book - 11

fashion umbrella - 12

how to use this book - 13

2 **fashion computing tool kit - 14**

intro - 15, apple mac or windows pc? - 15

table of software - 16, art box - 17

3 **computer basics - 18**

intro - 19, computer training - 19, file management - 19

bitmaps and vectors - 20, resolution - 21

image modes (RGB, CMYK, grayscale, duotone, bitmap mode) - 22

layers - 23, channels - 23

saving files - 24, file formats - 24

removable media - 25, printing color - 25, windows and mac - 25

4 **drawing techniques - 26**

fashion industry drawing software - 27, table of exercises - 27

work area - 28

Illustrator tools - 29

CorelDRAW tools - 30, Freehand tools - 30

terminology - 31

20 key fashion drawing techniques (drawing exercises) - 32 to 43

5 **flats and specs women - 44**

intro - 45, table of exercises - 45, flats/working drawings - 45

female croquis (figure template) - 46

tank top (stretch fabric) - 48, top with sleeves (stretch fabric) - 50

fitted shirt - 52, style variations - 53

fitted skirt (pencil) - 56, style variations - 57

fitted pant - 60, style variations - 61

fitted dress - 64, style variations - 65, design details - 66

specs (specification sheets) - 68

library of styles - 71

6 **menswear - 72**

intro - 73, table of exercises - 73, menswear styling - 73, male croquis (figure template) - 73

single breasted jacket - 74, jackets - 75

shirts - 76

pants - 77

7 **childrenswear - 78**

intro - 79, table of childrenswear flats - 79, childrenswear presentation - 79

babies rompers and dungarees - 80, kids swims - 80

kids bodysuits and jackets - 81

dresses - 82, skirts - 82, tops, shirts and blouses - 83

8 **scanning and digital photography - 84**

intro - 85, scanning tips - 85

digital photography tips - 87, digitised images - 87

9 **photoshop essential tools - 88**

intro - 89, table of exercises - 89

work area - 90, photoshop toolbox - 91

10 key fashion image editing techniques, photoshop exercises - 92 to 105

10 **photoshop color and effects - 106**

intro - 107, table of exercises - 107

11 key photoshop exercises, color and effects - 108 to 121

11 **design presentations - 122**

intro - 123, table of presentations and exercises - 123, 8 hot tips - 124

creating presentations - 125, design presentation exercises - 126 to 135

gallery of design presentations - 136 to 151

12 **digital portfolio - 152**

design portfolio - 153, plan your digital design portfolio - 153

create a powerpoint presentation -154

1 **appendix 1: cad - 156**

intro - 157

lectra cad suite - 158

cad apparel software - 160

2 **appendix 2: fashion internet - 162**

intro - 162

fashion sites - 163

further reading - 164

glossary - 166

index - 170

books by burke publishing- 174

authors note

who should use this book

Fashion Computing is essential reading for all enterprising fashion designers and fashion illustrators, and especially for aspiring students who wish to enter the world of fashion and design.

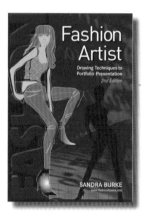

Fashion Artist - Drawing Techniques to Portfolio Presentation is the first book in my *Fashion Design Series* and has become established text in Universities and Fashion Schools internationally.

Instructor's Manual

An Instructor's Manual for lecturers is available at www.burkepublishing.com

The latest computer technology is having a huge impact on the way fashion designs are being created. Powerful graphics software offers the fashion designer simple tools and techniques to digitally produce their fashion designs, together with the capability to communicate electronically with the fashion industry internationally. Consequently, this digital revolution has developed a growing market for enterprising fashion designers and illustrators with creative computing skills.

Fashion schools have responded to the demand for fashion computing by including fashion computing modules within their fashion courses. These fashion computing modules are designed to give the students a thorough grounding in the computing skills required by the fashion industry.

With such dynamic changes in technology within the industry, I realised there was a need for a graphically presented text book to demystify fashion computing. *Fashion Computing - Design Techniques and CAD* is the first book to offer a comprehensive introduction to fashion computing design techniques, from drawing a simple basic bodice to creating dynamic design presentations and a digital design portfolio. *Fashion Computing* has been designed as a self-teaching book both for the novice and those who wish to enhance their fashion computing design skills.

In writing this book I have combined my career in fashion design, education and publishing – each discipline supporting the other. The result is a combination of the educational requirements of fashion programmes with the practical application of fashion computing design techniques used in the fashion industry.

The fashion industry, I know, is a challenging and competitive business and, therefore, it is essential for the budding fashion designer and fashion illustrator to be well equipped with professional fashion computing skills. The aim of *Fashion Computing* is to inspire you to develop these skills and achieve that *X-factor*. To be a successful designer you will need to work hard to develop your talent, believe in your own judgement, and have a certain amount of chutzpah! I wish you every success in the world of fashion.

Sandra Burke
M.Des RCA
(Master of Design, Royal College of Art)

foreword

When Sandra invited me to write the foreword to her second book in her *Fashion Design Series* I was delighted. Having known Sandra for over ten years I was conscious of her entrepreneurial qualities and her books on fashion illustration and design are no exception. Her first book, *Fashion Artist* has been very successful, and a great resource to students of fashion at all stages of their education.

Sandra's book on Fashion Computing is a natural progression both for the author, and for any student studying fashion. There are not many images these days that have not been manipulated or enhanced by the hand of technology, and many students are very keen to be able to master some of the techniques available to them through IT, to ensure their competitive edge.

Scanning, digitising, flood filling, colour and texture, manipulation, blending drawings and photographs and design work are all tasks that are now second nature to our fashion students, techniques that when we were students did not enter our consciousness, or our portfolios.

Whilst I am also quite convinced that the pencil is not redundant, the art of visually communicating fashion concepts and ideas through a range of media has always been a requisite of the design process. The power of the drawn image will not diminish, computer technology has only added to that range of media. I am sure, this book will be as useful to the teacher and design lecturer, as to the student of fashion.

Lucy Jones MA
Subject Director Fashion Textiles
University of East London

Lucy Jones on one of her business trips in Hong Kong, buying the latest digital camera as part of the digital fashion revolution!

acknowledgements

The research for *Fashion Computing - Design Techniques and CAD* has taken me to some of the most influential fashion companies and fashion schools around the world and further established the link between industry and education.

Initially I wish to thank all those who contributed to the content of this book. The sharing of ideas, encouragement and support from the fashion industry, lecturers, colleagues and friends from around the world has been absolutely incredible. I would never have been able to write this book without them. My sincere thanks to you all.

fashion industry
Amanda Lang, *Gerber Technology,* Australia
Crispin Scott, *Ted Baker,* London
Dave Edgar, *Bureaux Design,* London
David Shilling, *Creative Director,* London
Debbie Minné, *Chelsea West,* Cape Town
Francis Shilling, *Knitwear Designer,* London
Greg Pool, *GMT,* NZ
Jeremy Brandrick, Designer, *Marks and Spenser,* London
Judy Cimdins, *Beales,* UK
Laurie Dreyer, *Chelsea West,* Cape Town
Maria Leeke, *Marks & Spencer,* London
Michael Terry, *Dewhirst Group,* London,
Paul Rider, M.Des RCA, *Fashion Designer and Consultant,* London
Peter Flowers, *Foschini,* Cape Town
Design and Marketing Team, *Pumpkin Patch,* NZ and Australia
Ricki and Aviva Wolman, *Citron,* Santa Monica, LA
Tim Rathbone, *Beales,* UK
Francis Hooper and Denise L'Estrange, *World,* NZ
Yvonne Badcock, *Lectra Pty Ltd,* NZ

fashion illustrators and fashion designers
Alissa Stytsenko-Berdnik, *fashion designer and illustrator,* NZ
Bindi Learmont, *fashion illustrator,* Australia
Christopher Davies, *graphics and textile designer,* NZ
Frances Howie, *fashion designer for Lanvin,* Paris
Kashmir Kaur, *fashion designer,* UK
Jonathan Kyle Farmer ma(rca), *fashion designer/illustrator,* London
Joseph Kim, *fashion designer and illustrator,* NZ
Linda Logan, *fashion designer and Illustrator,* Cape Town
Lynnette Cook, *fashion illustrator,* London
Naomi Austin, *fashion illustrator,* UK
Stuart McKenzie, *fashion illustrator,* London
Susan Stoddart, *fashion designer,* UK

photographers

Michael Ng, International

Louise Davies, *fashion designer and photographer,* International

models

Esther Simmonds, International

Grace, agency 62, NZ

universities and fashion schools

Karen Scheetz, *Fashion Institute of Technology,* New York

Timothy Gunn, *Parsons School of Design,* New York

Lucy Jones, *University of East London,* London

Karen Singleton, *University of Bradford*

Michele Danjoux, *Nottingham Trent University*

Carolyn Livesey, *Northbrook University,* Sussex

Jan Hamon, *Costume Designer,* AUT, NZ

Mandy Smith, *Head of Fashion and Knitwear designer,* AUT, NZ

Lize Niemczyk, *Fashion Designer,* AUT, NZ

Lyle Reilly, *Fashion and Computing,* AUT, NZ

Sharon Evans-Mikellis, *Fashion designer,* AUT, NZ

And not forgetting the *Royal College of Art and Harrow (University of Westminster)* for giving me a fabulous education in fashion design.

dtp

Writing this book was one challenge, but becoming a complete technocrat and setting it up in color on InDesign was another. Particular thanks to Alan Taylor, Brian Farley, Bert Parsons, Simon Larkin, Rory Birk for their technical input.

proof reading

Thank you to my proof reading team; Jan Hamon, Alan Taylor, Lize Niemczyk and Rory Burke.

foreword

I particularly wish to thank Lucy Jones, *Director Fashion Textiles (UEL)* for her inspirational foreword.

Fashion Illustration by **Naomi Austin**

Created in Illustrator and Photoshop

getting started

Fashion Illustration by **Lynnette Cook**
Ink on paper, scanned illustrations, filled with
color and pattern in CorelDRAW

A techno revolution is taking place in the world of fashion - the introduction of powerful yet inexpensive computers and graphics software is encouraging fashion designers to use this exciting medium to create their fashion designs and presentations.

Graphics software, which includes drawing, image editing, page layout and web design, offers a multitude of tools and techniques. The designer can use these programs to sketch a simple technical line drawing of a basic tank top or a highly detailed jacket, create the most amazing fashion illustrations, and develop dynamic presentations and page layouts for print and screen.

The computer is a powerful tool, an extension of your hand, and an aid to your creativity and visualisation. Graphics software adds another perspective to your work with a wide range of techniques for creative design development and presentation. Combining your hand drawings and digitised visuals adds even more scope for innovation and personal style.

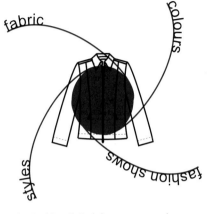

The Fashion Spiral demonstrates the elements that influence the creation of a fashion design. Image created in CorelDRAW

history

CAD/CAM (Computer-Aided Design and Computer-Aided Manufacturing) was introduced into the fashion industry in the 1980s as a stand-alone system. It was originally developed for the Textile and Apparel Industry as part of the manufacturing and production process, which included creating textiles, drafting and grading patterns. During this period, the graphics and media industries (advertising and publishing) were using computers and graphics software for their creative design work and media layouts.

More recently, graphics software has been integrated into the fashion design process to create technical drawings of designs as flats, specification drawings, fashion illustrations and design presentations. This has speeded up the design process and presents a global standard for the visual communication of designs to the production, manufacturing and marketing areas of the industry.

the aim of this book

Fashion Computing - Design Techniques and CAD introduces you to the computer drawing and design skills required by the fashion industry worldwide. Through visuals and easy steps, it explains how to use the most popular graphics software used in the fashion business. It demonstrates fashion drawing, design and presentation techniques and explains how to develop digital communications using powerful computerised tools. *Fashion Computing* will clearly demonstrate how your computer skills can be applied to the world of fashion and the fashion design process.

Design Presentation, hand drawn illustrations, scanned image of the Eiffel Tower, edited in Photoshop, by Susan Stoddart, Bradford College

the fashion computing umbrella

Fashion Computing - Design Techniques and CAD will take you through the following computing techniques:

- Design clothing as flats/working drawings
- Create specification/technical sheets for samples and production
- Create fashion illustrations and fabrics
- Create fashion presentations - mood/concept/theme, fabric, color, design, illustration, trend forecasting etc.
- Design promotional material for websites, marketing and branding, business cards and logos.

To make the most of this book you should have some basic fashion drawing and computing skills.

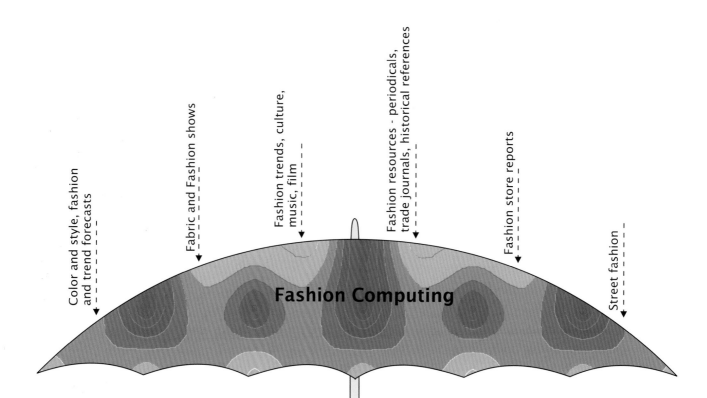

Color and style, fashion and trend forecasts

Fabric and Fashion shows

Fashion trends, culture, music, film

Fashion resources - periodicals, trade journals, historical references

Fashion store reports

Street fashion

Fashion Computing

| Flats | Illustration | Photography | Presentations | Forecasting | Promotion |

The Fashion Umbrella captures the scope of fashion computing from initial concept through to advertising and marketing

how to use this book

The chapters have been set out in a logical learning sequence to guide you through the computerised fashion design and presentation techniques, together with self-explanatory worked examples.

Chapter 2: Computer Tool Kit - discusses the 'tools of the trade', the hardware and software packages used in the fashion industry internationally.

Chapter 3: Computer Basics - discusses basic theory and terminology of computer graphics providing a useful reference as you work through the chapters.

Chapter 4: Drawing Techniques - demonstrates the techniques fashion designers use to draw flats using graphics drawing software, particularly Illustrator (Adobe), CorelDRAW, and Freehand (Macromedia).

Chapter 5: Flats and Specs Women - demonstrates how to draw flats for womenswear by applying the key fashion drawing techniques covered in the previous chapter.

Chapter 6: Menswear - demonstrates how to draw flats for menswear by applying the key fashion drawing techniques covered in the previous chapters.

Chapter 7: Childrenswear - demonstrates how to draw flats for childrenswear by applying the key fashion drawing techniques covered in the previous chapters.

Chapter 8: Scanning and Digital Photography - explains how fashion designers scan and digitise images as part of the design process.

Chapter 9: Photoshop Essential Tools - demonstrates how to use the essential image editing techniques, tools and commands to edit and enhance fashion designs and illustrations.

Chapter 10: Photoshop Color and Effects – demonstrates how to use the key image editing techniques for working with color and pattern, and how to develop creative effects.

Chapter 11: Design Presentations - demonstrates how to use Photoshop to create professional fashion design presentations.

Chapter 12: Digital Design Portfolio - discusses how to develop a digital design portfolio using PowerPoint which can be used for 'live' presentations, saved on disc and published to the World Wide Web.

Appendix 1: Fashion CAD - discusses the CAD giants of the apparel and textile industry - Gerber and Lectra.

Appendix 2: Fashion Internet - lists useful fashion websites on the World Wide Web.

Further Reading, Glossary, and Index

Computer generated images from designers and illustrators around the world have been included to inspire you and to demonstrate fashion computing techniques.

Fashion Computing offers you the skills and techniques to catch the wave of the latest technology. This will be your competitive advantage in a constantly developing and exciting market place - the World of Fashion!

'African Theme' illustrations hand drawn, edited in Photoshop and Illustrator - created by Alissa Stytsenko-Berdnik

© Fashion Computing - Sandra Burke

2
fashion computing toolkit

Fashion Presentation by **Yatika Keshav**
*Digital photographs, scanned images
and fabrics, edited in Freehand and
Photoshop*

Fashion computing requires specific graphics software to produce marketable fashion designs for print and screen. This chapter introduces you to the most popular hardware and software programs used internationally in the Fashion Industry, and discusses your options.

As computers become more powerful but less expensive there is something to fit every budget. Technology is constantly being updated so it is important to get the latest information, for example:

• Discuss your options with your lecturer/computer trainer, and the vendor

• Search on-line – check out software packages, computers, digital cameras, prices, ratings, advice, tips etc.

• Read computer magazines - although aimed at computer geeks, there are always useful snippets of information for the novice as well

• Enquire as to what software is being supported by the local fashion industries.

apple mac or windows pc?

Apple Mac was the first company to develop professional interactive graphics software and was considered to have set the market standard system for graphic design. As technology has developed, identical graphics software is now available for both Windows PC and Mac - it has subsequently become a question of personal preference. (This book was written using both PC and Mac computers.)

computer software

The vast choice of computer software can be confusing. However, there are a number of packages which have become universally accepted in the fashion and graphics industries, for example:

• **Microsoft Office** - Word, Excel, PowerPoint

• **Graphics (Drawing) packages** - Illustrator (Adobe), CorelDRAW, or Freehand (Macromedia) (each country and industry has a preferred package, although once you learn how to use one package it is easy to learn another)

• **Image Editing program** - Photoshop (Adobe).

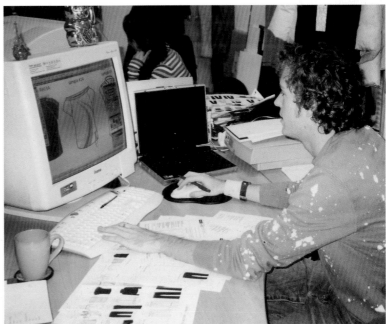

A fashion designer working at a typical fashion graphics work station - a desktop computer, laptop, scanner, keyboard, and mouse. The only items missing are a digital camera, Wacom graphics tablet and printer - courtesy of Dewhirst, London

software	description
Microsoft Office includes: Word, Excel, PowerPoint, Publisher	**Microsoft Word** (word processing) - creates text documents, spec sheets **Excel** – creates spreadsheets, use for spec sheets where tables and flats are required **PowerPoint** - creates presentations for screen (slide show/video/web/email attachments) **Publisher** - basic publishing, good starting point for introduction to graphics.
Drawing Software: Illustrator, CorelDRAW, Freehand	Powerful graphics drawing programs - excellent for drawing lines and shapes to create flats/working drawings and technical drawings for specification sheets, including fashion illustrations and presentation work (import images e.g. photos, scans etc.).
Image Editing Software: Photoshop	Industry standard software for image editing, a powerful paint and photo editing program - import, edit and manipulate scanned/digital images, or create images from the initial concept. Images created in drawing packages can be brought into Photoshop to create impressive fashion and fabric presentations for printing and the Web.
Page Layout: QuarkXpress, In-Design (Adobe)	Industry standard for advertising and publishing to produce quality page layout - create dynamic layouts for magazines, brochures, promotional material, marketing etc. (*Fashion Computing's* cover was designed using Photoshop and QuarkXpress, and the content created using InDesign.)
Web Design: Dreamweaver (Fireworks, Flash), Front Page, Image Ready (Photoshop)	Dreamweaver - powerful software for web design (Flash - excellent for creating animations for a more dynamic website. Fireworks for web graphics - also part of the Freehand, Dreamweaver, Flash package) Image Ready (Photoshop) - create and optimize web graphics
Adobe Acrobat	Excellent for converting large image files into PDFs to send as email attachments - on receipt the PDF can be edited, notes attached etc., and emailed back or forwarded. Acrobat Reader (free download) for on screen reading of PDFs.
Winzip (Windows), **Stuffit** (Mac)	Excellent for compressing files ('zip' or 'stuff'), then send the files as email attachments - the receiver must have Winzip or Stuffit to open the files.
Creative Suites: Adobe, CorelDRAW, Macromedia	Graphics Suites (include Drawing, Image Editing, Page Layout and Web Design Software) are less expensive compared to purchasing each package individually.
CAD Suites: Primavision (Lectra), Artworks (Gerber)	Software Suites designed to meet the specific needs of the Apparel and Textile Industry - used primarily in fashion companies, with long production runs, for fashion and textile design, pattern making, grading, manufacturing, labelling, etc.
Fashion Specific: Fashion Studio, Guided Image, Speedstep etc.	There are several Fashion and Textile design specific packages available for fashion design and presentation work which are less expensive than the more powerful CAD specialist suites - check compatibility with in-house systems, outside printers and service bureaus.

Figure 2.1:
This table describes the software used in the fashion industry.

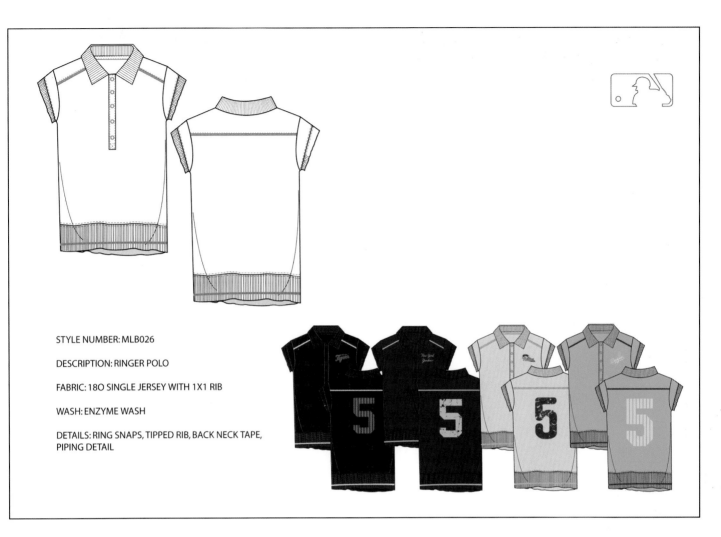

Fashion Design Presentation by **Bureaux Design**, *London*

STYLE NUMBER: MLB026

DESCRIPTION: RINGER POLO

FABRIC: 180 SINGLE JERSEY WITH 1X1 RIB

WASH: ENZYME WASH

DETAILS: RING SNAPS, TIPPED RIB, BACK NECK TAPE, PIPING DETAIL

art box

Computers have not completely taken over - yet! The fashion designer still needs to develop hand drawing design skills to be a cut above the competition. To complement your computer kit, your art box should consist of art paper, colouring media, sketchbooks and a portfolio for your finished work, For more information see my book, *Fashion Artist - Drawing Techniques to Portfolio Presentation.*

Now you are ready to power up your computer, join the *technocrats* and enter the exciting cyber world of fashion!

3

computer basics

*Fashion Presentation by **Rory O'Dea***
Digital photographs, scanned fabric, body mapping
software, edited in Freehand and Photoshop

This chapter introduces important computer topics and terminology which apply to all graphics software - you will find this a useful reference as you work through the chapters.

computer training

If you do not have the basic computing skills such as opening and saving files, standard menus and using a mouse, help is at hand. There are numerous introductory courses offered by local institutes; libraries, community centres and schools, at either no charge or a minimal fee. These courses include: Introduction to Computers, Microsoft Word, Microsoft Excel, Microsoft PowerPoint, Internet, Email, Creating Websites. Some of the basic skills and techniques taught are:

• Creating and opening folders and files, file (new, close, save, print), editing (cut, copy, paste, select all), spell check, undo, redo, find, search.

file management

As you progress through the exercises in *Fashion Computing* you will create numerous image files and require an efficient filing system for finding and saving files. For example, create a folder called **Fashion Designs**, then create subfolders for further categories which may include (see image of folders below):

• **Croquis** folder, containing all figure croquis/templates

• **Flats** folder containing subfolders of your designs for women, men, children, trends and, within those subfolders, folders for tops, shirts, pants, jackets, etc.

• **Library of Styles** folder, containing subfolders of silhouettes; skirt shapes, dress shapes, collar shapes, etc.

• **Photos and Scans** folder for scans and digital photographs and subfolders for Moods/Themes (Texture, Architecture, Culture, Music, 60s, 70s), Fabric/ Color scans (Stripes, Checks, Florals, Woollens, Brights, Pastels).

• **Presentations** folder, containing a folder for each presentation - Menswear Retro Mood Board, Sportswear Flats, Urban Safari Fabric Presentation, etc.

Help! - if you hit a problem e.g. you are unsure how to use a tool, or you have forgotten where to find a particular command, use the 'Help' (Menu Bar) - the more you use it the easier technical issues become.

'Thumbnail' view is an excellent way to view and look for image files.

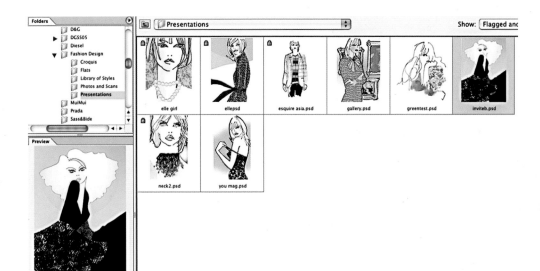

bitmaps and vectors

Graphics software works with images either as 'Vectors' or 'Bitmaps';

• Drawing packages, such as Illustrator, CorelDRAW, and Freehand, create 'Vector' images which are images created using smooth lines and curves.

• Image Editing software, such as Photoshop, edits and manipulates 'Bitmap' images which are created from pixels (a rectangular grid/raster of pixels). A bitmap image is created when you scan a photograph, fashion illustration or fabric swatch, etc, or take a photograph using a digital camera.

vector images;

• Are created by a mathematical formula which forms smooth lines and curves which are 'resolution independent' (see image below)

• 'Resolution independent' images may be scaled up or down without deterioration, and remain sharp and clear

• Make excellent line drawings such as; flats and specification drawings, logos, T-shirt images for sportswear, etc.

• Are much smaller in file size compared to bitmap files - this makes flats and specs ideal to send as email attachments in their native file format (e.g. Illustrator file) and, once downloaded, they can be scaled to the required size.

bitmap images;

• Are measured as dpi (dots per inch) and are 'resolution dependant' which means that if an image is scaled up, the pixels get larger and the image will become less clear with jagged edges

• Are edited in image editing software (Photoshop) - when you edit a bitmap image you are actually editing each pixel or group of pixels

• Are edited in image editing software to create montages/collaged storyboards and fashion design presentations

• For the best results, scan and work in image editing software at the correct resolution and size from the outset.

Vectors can be 'placed' in Image Editing programs e.g. place a flat created in Illustrator into a Photoshop Presentation; Bitmaps can be placed in Drawing programs e.g. edit a scanned fashion illustration in Photoshop and place it in a presentation created in Illustrator.

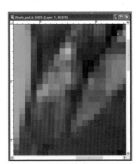

Zoom in on a Bitmap image to see each pixel and how they form a rectangular grid/raster of pixels

actual size   **scaled up**

Vector drawing at actual size, and scaled up - note the lines remain smooth and clear

resolution

The resolution of an image is a key factor when working on bitmap images. Before scanning an image, taking a digital photograph, or creating a 'new file' in an image editing program (Photoshop), the required resolution and image mode (RGB, CMYK, Grayscale) should be determined.

For the resolution choose:

• 300 dpi for commercial printing of books, glossy magazines, brochures

• 150 - 200 dpi for laser and inkjet printers (home/office printers); make a test print to clarify the best resolution for your printer

• 72 - 96 dpi for email attachments, the web, PowerPoint and multimedia.

Scanned at 30 dpi

 Resolution (dpi) can be changed in Photoshop. While minor changes in resolution are acceptable, major changes will cause loss of detail and color.

 For a digital camera - the greater the dpi, the better the photograph for detail and color.

Scanned at 100 dpi

 For commercial publishing you should discuss the requirements with your printer or service bureaux.

Scanned at 300 dpi

RGB image converted to CMYK for commercial printing (book, mag)

RGB Image converted to Grayscale

Duotone image using two colors, red and pink

Image converted to bitmap mode, with 50% Threshold option

image modes

As you work with graphics software you will primarily work in RGB mode, but you also need to be aware of the other image modes.

RGB (Red, Green, Blue);

• The most common mode for working with color images - photographs, fashion drawings and illustrations for general printing and web/screen

• Is faster to work with than CMYK, as RGB creates a smaller file size (for this reason, if your image is for commercial printing, convert to CMYK once all changes have been made to the image)

• The human eye perceives color as RGB; scanners and digital cameras capture color information in RGB; computer monitors display color as RGB

• Mixing RGB in varying proportions produces millions of different colors - the absence of white light creates black; while the complete saturation of light creates white; equal amounts of red, green and blue create intermediate shades of gray.

CMYK (Cyan, Magenta, Yellow, Black);

• RGB images must be converted to CMYK for commercial printing e.g. glossy magazines and brochures, where color separations are required for commercial offset printing (inkjet printers tend to be CMYK, but do not print such fine quality)

• When an image is converted to CMYK some of the brilliance of the RGB gamut (range) of colors will be lost, so the image will have a duller appearance.

Grayscale;

• Grayscale images include actual shades of gray - the pixels are made up of white, gray and black. 256 levels of gray will represent most black and white photos accurately

• You can convert a color image to grayscale, but not back again to a color image.

Duotone;

• You can convert a grayscale image to a duotone (two colors) - duotone is an easy way to add color to a black and white photograph - choose black and a color, two colors or, even tritone (three inks), or quadtone (four inks). (Beware, duotones will not print correctly on some printers.)

Bitmap Mode;

• Bitmap mode images are made up of black and white pixels with no shades of gray or color.

• Line drawings scanned on a scanner in 'line mode' are bitmap images consisting only of black and white pixels.

 NOTE *The term 'bitmap' is used to describe any image made up of pixels. There is also a file format called 'bitmap' abbreviated to BMP (.bmp).*

layers

Typically, you work in multiple layers when using graphics software. Layers allow you to keep elements in the image separate so that each layer can be edited separately. This is especially useful when working with complex images with many elements e.g. a fashion design presentation.

Layers can be;

- Created and deleted (each new layer adds to the file size)
- Duplicated
- Named and renamed
- Moved up or down to rearrange the sequence
- Linked, hidden, locked, merged into each other to help consolidate multi-layers
- Edited and manipulated - change the transparency, opacity, blending modes, create drop shadows (Photoshop) etc.
- Transformed: scaled, rotated, distorted etc.

The **Layers palette** displays each layer, its properties, and is used to edit and manipulate layers.

- A thumbnail of the image is displayed in each layer
- An eye icon indicates the layer is displayed
- A highlighted layer means the layer is 'active'
- A brush icon indicates the layer can be edited
- A padlock icon indicates the layer is locked and cannot be edited
- An 'f' symbol indicates a layer effect has been applied to the layer

Flatten - when all the changes have been made to an image it can then be flattened - this creates a single background layer. Flattening reduces the file size and is absolutely necessary for some file formats e.g. PICT, GIF, BMP, JPEG, Tiff and EPS, but it means that all the images are now on one layer and cannot be edited and moved as easily as before. It is good practise to also save a copy of the original unflattened version before you flatten an image. If the image needs further editing you can do this with more flexibility in the unflattened version.

channels

Although I do not discuss using channels in this book, it is a word you will come across when working with graphics software. In Photoshop, the **Channels palette** displays the current make up of the color elements in the image. By default, in RGB mode, there are three channels, one for each color (red, green and blue); in CMYK mode there are four channels, one for each color (cyan, magenta, yellow, and black); Indexed Color mode, Grayscale mode, and Bitmap mode, all have one channel. Additional channels can be added and are displayed e.g. the composite image (all the channels/colors which make up the image combined).

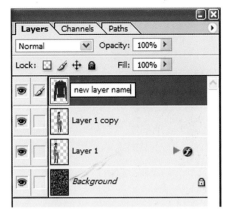

Photoshop Layers palette - the background layer is the first layer created, new layers can be created, copied and named

Layers can be dragged to new positions - here the shirt has been positioned below Layer 1 and Layer 1 copy

The layers have been flattened so only the background remains

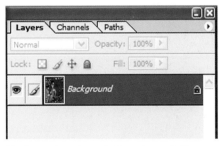

The Channels palette displays the Red, Green and Blue channels, plus a composite channel, RGB, of all three colors

© Fashion Computing - Sandra Burke

saving files

It is good practice to save your work at regular intervals:

- Use 'Save' or 'Save As'. Files automatically save in their native file format (the format of the particular package where the image is created) e.g. Photoshop (.psd), .ai (Illustrator)

- Make all changes to the image in its native format before you 'save' or 'export' to another format (non native) - non native formats are required when a file needs to be opened in another application e.g. for a page layout, a PowerPoint presentation, for a Website, or for email as an attachment

- To save a file in a non native format choose File>Save As, or File>Export (to display a dialog box with file options).

file formats

There are numerous graphics file formats for saving an image, Fig. 3.1 explains the formats you are most likely to use in the fashion industry.

file type	extension	use for	information
PSD (Photoshop - native image format)	.psd	Photoshop images	Retains layers - this is the best format if you still need to make changes to your images
AI (Illustrator) CDR (CorelDRAW) FH (Freehand) (Native image formats)	.ai .cdr .fh	Illustrator images CorelDRAW images Freehand images	Creates a small file size (can send as an attachment but the receiver must have the identical software to be able to read the file), once downloaded the 'vector' image can be scaled up or down as required
TIFF	.tif, .tiff	Scanned images (photographs, magazine clippings, illustrations and flats)	Universal graphics format supported by most graphics software; word processing, page layout software - supports layers but images are best flattened to create a smaller file size
EPS	.eps	Vector images	Universal graphics file format supported by most graphics software (will only print the 'preview' on non postscript printers e.g. inkjets)
JPEG	.jpeg, .jpg	Color and grayscale digital images (design presentations, photographs)	Use for the Web and email attachments; creates a very small file size by compression (keep a master copy as JPEG compression causes quality losses each time it is saved). (Unsuitable for images with solid blocks of color e.g. line drawings)
GIF	.gif	Illustrations with solid colors e.g. logos	Use for the Web, also supports animation, creates a very small file size by compression
PDF	.pdf	Illustration and text documents	Use for the Web, email attachments and commercial printing. Read files using Acrobat Reader (free download) which means that you do not need the original program to read the file.

Figure 3.1

This table describes the most common file formats used in the fashion industry.

removable media

To create backup files and avoid the risk of losing your data, or to transfer images to another computer, there are several medias to choose from:

- **CD-R** - write to once, cannot erase to free up space - holds 650MB of data

- **CD-RW** - rewrite and erase data up to a thousand times - holds 650MB of data

- **DVD+R** - use for data and DVD / film, write to once - holds 4.7GB of data

- **DVD+RW / DVD-RW -** data and DVD / film, rewrite - holds 4.7GB of data

- **Memory / data stick -** more expensive, plugs into a USB port, copy and erase endless times, different storage sizes available, extremely small in size

- **Portable hard drives** are popular but expensive, depending on storage capacity. You can create, save your files, or copy/mirror your hard drive as a disaster recovery response to a hard-drive crash.

Memory/data stick plugged into the USB port of a laptop

Portable hard drive plugged into the USB port of a laptop

printing color

Your monitor displays color as RGB; from device to device (scanner, to computer monitor to printer) colors will inevitably change. Most inkjet printers use four (CMYK) to six color inks to print an image, consequently the brightness of the RGB image on the monitor will be lost once printed. Even with commercial printing, it is difficult to achieve exact color matches. To get the best quality and closest color match for your print job use:

- The best quality printer available to you

- The correct paper for the job - there are a wide variety of paper types and qualities for printing e.g. standard inkjet paper, photographic paper, glossy paper

- The correct printer settings to match the print job

- Try printing your color images in both RGB and CMYK to check which is the best result for the job.

To find out more search on the Internet - you will find a vast amount of information on the best media to use and techniques of how to get the best print.

windows and mac

The two dominant computer platforms are Apple Mac and Windows PC. You could find yourself working between the two platforms e.g. at work or university you could be using a Mac, and at home, a PC. Mac and PC work with many similar commands but there are a few differences which will be useful to know when working through the exercises in this book:

- **Ctrl** (Windows) - **Apple** and **Command** (Mac)

- **Alt** (Windows) - **alt/option** (Mac)

- **Shift** is standard on both Platforms

- **To access context sensitive menus:** Windows users use the right mouse - Mac users can hold down the Control key and press their single mouse button

swapping files - You can read your files on either system providing that when using a Mac you save your files on PC formatted media and with a file extension. A PC can only read PC formatted media and requires the file extension so that it can recognise which program to use to open the file e.g. clothing**.ai** (Illustrator), clothing**.psd** (Photoshop), clothing**.cdr** (CorelDRAW) etc. (see Fig. 3.1). Macs automatically recognise which program to open a file therefore do not need file extensions. Fonts will need to be substituted if you do not have the same ones on your system, but all images can be opened.

Care must be taken when changing platforms (Mac - PC) as there are subtle differences between programs - even the same version could create problems. It is therefore not recommended that you regularly change platforms with the same file.

NOTE

4

drawing
techniques

Fashion Illustration by **Lynnette Cook**
Created in CorelDRAW

fashion industry drawing software

In the fashion industry, graphics drawing programs are increasingly being used by fashion designers as their electronic pencil and paper to draw clothing as flats/working drawings. Internationally, the three most popular graphics drawing programs are Illustrator, CorelDRAW, and Freehand.

NOTE *The techniques described here will apply to all drawing software*

This chapter explains how to use these three programs to draw flats using 20 key fashion drawing techniques, tools and commands. Fig. 4.1 presents an overview of these techniques and outlines the structure of this chapter. This is an excellent reference guide to refer to as you work through the following exercises and chapters. These techniques will be developed further in the *Flats and Specs* chapter.

techniques	exercises
1. Creating a New Image	1. Create a new blank image
2. Rulers and Guides	2. Show rulers and drag guides on to the work area
3. Drawing Lines (Strokes)	3a. Draw a straight line; 3b. Change stroke weights, create dashed lines
4. Drawing Flats	4. Draw a basic bodice
5. Selecting Objects (Flats)	5. Select and deselect the bodice
6. Selecting Anchor Points	6. Reshape the bodice armhole
7. Adding Anchor Points	7. Add an anchor point to the bodice
8. Deleting Anchor Points	8. Delete an anchor point from the bodice
9. Shaping Lines/Objects	9. Draw a zig-zag line and shape to make smooth curves
10. Shaping Flats	10. Select and curve the bodice neckline and armhole
11. Drawing Circles and Ovals (Buttons)	11. Create and align buttons on the centre front line of the bodice
12. Drawing Rectangles (Pockets)	12. Draw a pocket and topstitching, 'Group' and reposition it
13. Rotating Objects	13. Rotate the pocket on the bodice
14. Creating Text	14. Create a logo on the pocket
15. Zooming In and Out of an Image	15. Zoom in to view the pocket details
16. Scaling an Object Up or Down (Pocket)	16. Scale the bodice pocket up and down
17. Reflecting/Mirroring Objects (Flats)	17. Reflect the half bodice to create a complete bodice
18. Filling Objects (Flats) with Color	18. Fill the bodice/flat with color
19. Sending Objects to the Front or Back	19. Draw a sleeve and send it to the back of the bodice
20. Filling Objects (Flats) with a Gradient	20. Fill a bodice/flat with a gradient

Figure 4.1
Table of Drawing Techniques and Exercises

work area

The starting point for all drawing packages is the Work Area. All drawing software will have a similar arrangement to Figure 4.2 which is the Work Area from Illustrator. The drawing tools and commands for the techniques in this chapter are selected from the **Tool Box, Menu Bar** and the **Palettes** which appear within the Work Area.

menu bar (toolbar): displays Menu Commands - choose a command on the menu bar to display a dropdown list e.g. Choose View (Menu Bar)>Guides>Lock Guides.

palettes: display editing and monitoring options e.g. color (RGB, CMYK), swatches, brushes, stroke weight (line thickness), dashed lines, gradient, transparency, layers, align. To select a palette choose Window (Menu Bar) (a check mark next to the palette name indicates it is selected). These small windows can be moved around the Work Area.

toolbox: displays the drawing and editing tools as icons. Click on a tool to select it - a small triangle next to the tool icon indicates hidden tools - click on the triangle to open and select another tool. These hidden tools can be torn off/floated and moved around the work area - a useful feature for frequently used tools.

artboard: the area where the fashion drawing is created and edited.

status bar: displays information about the open document and the tool currently being used.

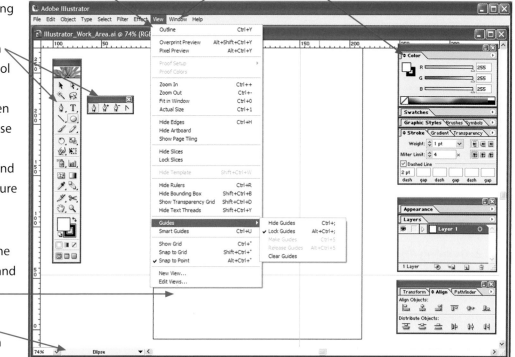

Figure 4.2
Work Area (Illustrator) displaying a typical drawing program layout with Menu Bar, Palettes, Toolbox, Artboard and Status Bar

 When you select a tool the mouse pointer changes to match the tool's icon.

 Position the pointer over a tool to display the tool's name and short-cut (short-cuts are great for tools most frequently used e.g. click 'Z' for the Zoom tool).

 ***Help!** - if you hit a problem or need more information use the Help (Menu Bar). It is a great reference guide and the more you use it the easier technical issues become.*

Illustrator

Toolbox and Hidden Tools (used in the exercises)

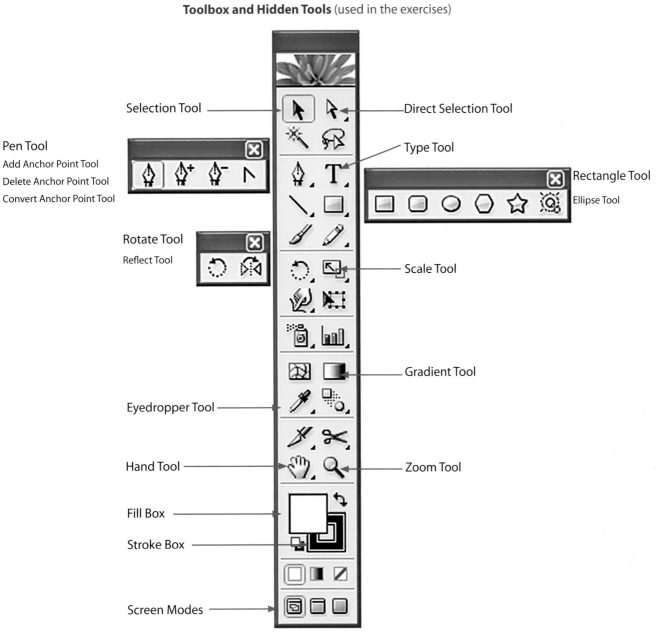

Selection Tool

Direct Selection Tool

Pen Tool

Add Anchor Point Tool

Delete Anchor Point Tool

Convert Anchor Point Tool

Type Tool

Rectangle Tool

Ellipse Tool

Rotate Tool

Reflect Tool

Scale Tool

Gradient Tool

Eyedropper Tool

Hand Tool

Zoom Tool

Fill Box

Stroke Box

Screen Modes

Stroke palette (Gradient and Transparency) - to display, choose Window (Menu Bar)>Stroke

Color palette (RGB)

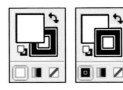

Figure 4.3

Exploded view of Illustrator's Toolbox and the hidden tools, palettes, Stroke and Fill Box used in the exercises

---

Stroke and Fill Box (default black stroke and white fill)

- Click on either box to swop between boxes

- To fill an object with white the fill box must have white selected

- To draw a black line the stroke box must have black selected

- A line through a box indicates that there is no stroke line or no fill in that particular box (the object will have no stroke or no fill)

- Click on the fill box and select a color from the color picker box

- Click on the stroke box and select a color from the color picker box

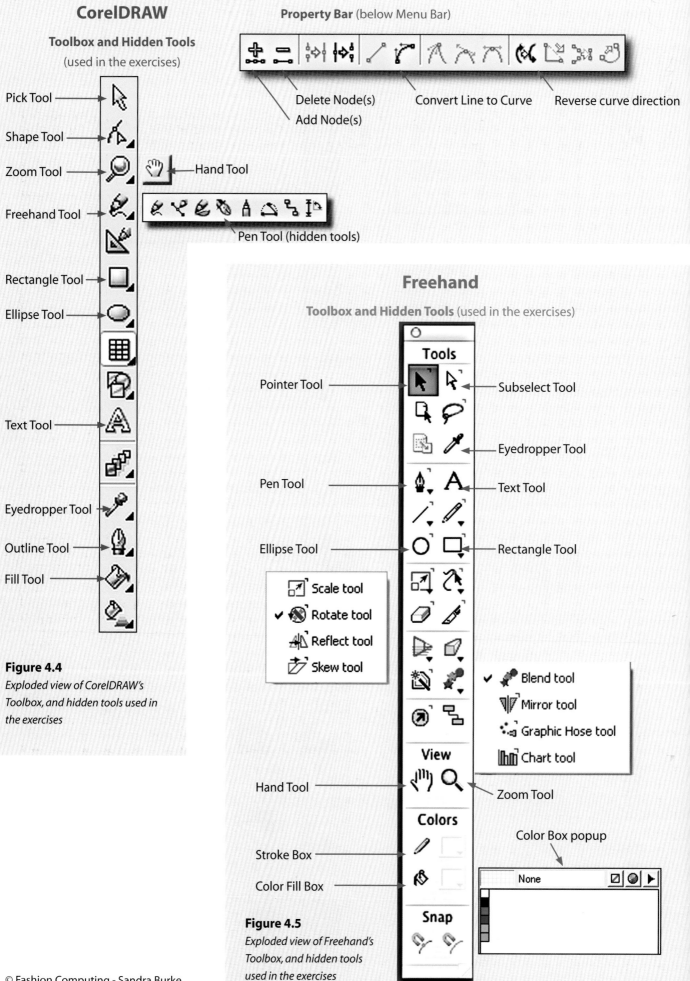

CorelDRAW

Toolbox and Hidden Tools
(used in the exercises)

Pick Tool
Shape Tool
Zoom Tool
Hand Tool
Freehand Tool
Pen Tool (hidden tools)
Rectangle Tool
Ellipse Tool
Text Tool
Eyedropper Tool
Outline Tool
Fill Tool

Figure 4.4
Exploded view of CorelDRAW's Toolbox, and hidden tools used in the exercises

Property Bar (below Menu Bar)

Delete Node(s)
Add Node(s)
Convert Line to Curve
Reverse curve direction

Freehand

Toolbox and Hidden Tools (used in the exercises)

Tools
Pointer Tool
Subselect Tool
Eyedropper Tool
Pen Tool
Text Tool
Ellipse Tool
Rectangle Tool

Scale tool
✓ Rotate tool
Reflect tool
Skew tool

✓ Blend tool
Mirror tool
Graphic Hose tool
Chart tool

View
Hand Tool
Zoom Tool

Colors
Color Box popup
Stroke Box
Color Fill Box
None

Snap

Figure 4.5
Exploded view of Freehand's Toolbox, and hidden tools used in the exercises

terminology

Fig. 4.6 compares the terminology used between the drawing packages. The terminology is listed in the same order as it is introduced in the exercises in this chapter. This table is an excellent reference guide as you work though the techniques.

Illustrator	CorelDRAW	Freehand
Work Area	Application Window	Document Window
Menu Bar	Menu Bar, Property Bar, Tool Bar	Menu, Toolbars
Palettes	Dockers	Panels
Artboard	Drawing Page	Document Page
Stroke	Outline	Stroke
Stroke Weight	Outline Width	Stroke Width
Anchor Point	Node	Point
Selection Tool	Pick Tool	Pointer Tool
Direct Selection Tool	Shape Tool	Pointer Tool
Add Anchor Point Tool	Shape Tool	Pointer Tool, Pen Tool
Delete Anchor Point Tool	Shape Tool	Pointer Tool, Pen Tool
Convert Anchor Point Tool	Shape Tool	Subselect Tool
Direction Handle	Control Point	Point Handles
Rotate Tool	Dockers>Transformations>Rotate	Rotate Tool
Type Tool	Text Tool	Text Tool
Type Palette	Property Bar	Text Bar
Scale Tool	Dockers>Transformations	Scale Tool
Reflect Tool	Dockers>Transformations	Mirror Tool
Fill and Stroke Boxes	Fill Tool, Outline Tool	Stroke and Color Fill Box
Color Palette, Swatches Palette	Color Palettes	Color Mixer, Swatches
Gradient	Fountain Fill (Interactive Fill)	Gradient
Place (Image)	Import (Image)	Import (Image)
Rasterize	Convert to a Bitmap	Rasterize

Figure 4.6

This table compares the terminology used by Illustrator, CorelDRAW and Freehand

 White 'fill' and black 'strokes' (lines) are the standard when drawing flats - however, color has been used here for clarity of the techniques.

 If an exercise is not working properly make sure you have selected the bodice/path correctly and are working with the correct tool.

20 key fashion drawing techniques

If you make a mistake press the delete key or, to go back to a previous state, choose Edit (Menu Bar)>Undo.

The following 20 key fashion drawing techniques are set out as step-by-step exercises based on a simple bodice. Key tools and commands are used to *'get you started'* and will be further developed in the next chapter, *Flats and Specs*. For this reason, no specific measurements are used in the exercises here.

1. creating a new image

Exercise 1: *Create a new blank image.*

- **Illustrator:** Choose File (Menu Bar)>New (the New dialog box appears)
- Type a name for the new image, enter page size etc.
- A new image window is created and the name appears in its title bar.

- **CorelDRAW:** Choose File (Menu Bar)>New (a new blank page appears)
- Select and enter page size etc. in the Property Bar.

- **Freehand:** Choose File (Menu)>New
- Choose Window (Menu)>Document (to display the Document panel), in the panel click the Document tab, select and enter page size etc.

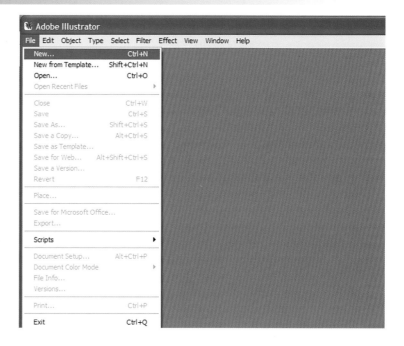

2. rulers and guides

Rulers and guides are used to enable precise positioning and alignment of elements e.g. positioning the centre front line to an exact point.

Rulers and guides are non-printing and can be displayed or hidden. Guides can also be selected or deselected to 'Lock', 'Clear', 'Snap to Point'.

Exercise 2: *Show rulers and drag guides onto the work area (the guides will be used to position anchor points for drawing the bodice).*

The rulers 'x' and 'y' show the measurements. Guides are the lines you drag out from the rulers and position onto the artboard.

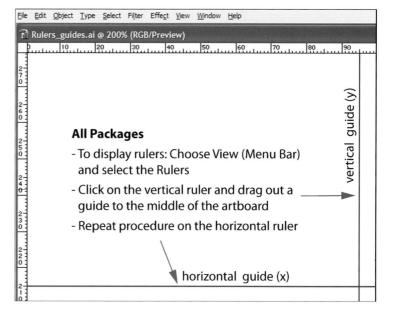

All Packages
- To display rulers: Choose View (Menu Bar) and select the Rulers
- Click on the vertical ruler and drag out a guide to the middle of the artboard
- Repeat procedure on the horizontal ruler

vertical guide (y)

horizontal guide (x)

3. drawing lines (strokes)

Illustrator: Pen Tool and Selection Tool

CorelDRAW: Pen Tool

Freehand: Pen Tool

This tool is used to create straight lines. Generally, black lines (strokes) with a 1 pt thickness (weight) are a suitable weight for drawing flats. Stroke lines can be different weights, dashed, coloured etc.

Exercise 3A: *Draw a straight line.*

Exercise 3B: *Change stroke weights, create dashed lines.*

Illustrator: Choose Window (Menu Bar)> Stroke (palette) and, in the palette, select Stroke attributes

CorelDRAW: Select from the Property Bar

Freehand: Choose Window (Menu)>Object (to display the Object panel), in the panel, select Stroke: Basic and select Stroke attributes.

Exercise 3A - All Packages
- Select the Pen Tool
- Click the tip of the Pen Tool on the horizontal guide to start the line - this creates anchor point 1
- Click further along the guide to create anchor point 2, continue clicking to create more anchor points
- To end the line (**Illustrator:** Select the Selection Tool) (**CorelDraw** and **Freehand:** Double click)
- To delete, press the delete key while the line is still selected or see exercise 5 to select, and delete the line.

guide   1 ☐━━━━━━━━━━━━━━━━━☐ 2   guide

Exercise B - All Packages

Note: The line must be selected before you can change its attributes

	stroke weight (thickness)	dashed line (length of dash)	
0.75 pt	_____	-----------------	2 pt
1 pt	_____	- - - - - - - - - -	3 pt
2 pt	━━━━━━━━━	·················	2 pt

4. drawing flats

Illustrator: Pen Tool

CorelDRAW: Pen Tool

Freehand: Pen Tool

This tool is excellent for drawing flats – your most useful and frequently used drawing tool.

Exercise 4: *Draw a basic bodice.*

All Packages
- Select the Pen Tool
- Place the first anchor point *1* on the centre front (neck position)
- Then create anchor points *2* to *7*
- (CorelDraw and Freehand: double click to end the path/line)
- **Illustrator:** Make sure colour 'fill' is on (default white) (see Illustrator Toolbox)
- **CorelDRAW** and **Freehand:** The path will be closed in the reflecting/mirroring objects exercise 17, then filled in exercise 18

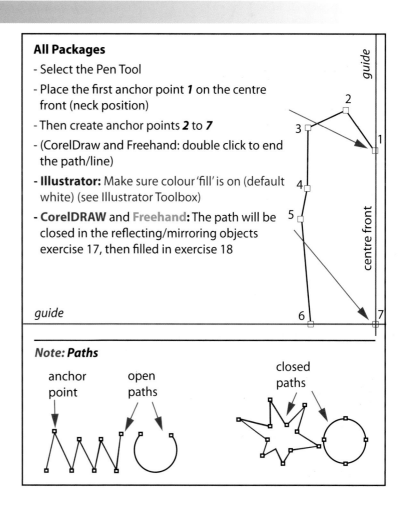

Note: Paths

anchor point   open paths   closed paths

Paths: *As you click and draw with the Pen Tool, anchor points are formed producing a 'path'. A 'path' can be 'open' (a line or shape with end points unconnected), or 'closed' (a circle or shape with ends connected).*

5. selecting objects (flats)

 Illustrator: Selection Tool

CorelDRAW: Pick Tool

Freehand: Pointer Tool

This tool is used to select objects (flats). A selected object can then be edited or moved e.g. change its attributes (line weight, color), move it to a different position on the artboard, rotate it, delete it, reshape it.

Exercise 5: *Select and deselect the bodice.*

 To select several components at once hold down 'shift' as you click each one.

 To view the image choose View (Menu Bar)>Fit in Window or Zoom etc., or use the horizontal and vertical scroll bars.

All Packages
- Select the tool for selecting objects
- To select the bodice click anywhere within the bodice

- To deselect the bodice click anywhere outside of the bodice

- *Note: When the bodice is selected, anchor points (and in Illustrator selection lines also) will appear indicating the selection has been made*

6. selecting anchor points

 Illustrator: Direct Selection Tool

CorelDRAW: Shape Tool

Freehand: Pointer Tool

This tool is used to select and move an anchor point on a path e.g. to edit the shape of a line (design) such as an armhole, neckline, sleeve, collar, waistband.

Exercise 6: *Reshape the bodice armhole.*

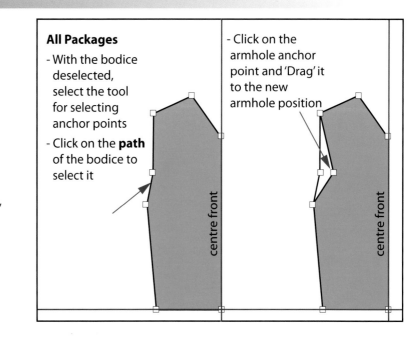

All Packages
- With the bodice deselected, select the tool for selecting anchor points
- Click on the **path** of the bodice to select it

- Click on the armhole anchor point and 'Drag' it to the new armhole position

7. adding anchor points

Illustrator: Add Anchor Point Tool and Direct Selection Tool

CorelDRAW: Shape Tool and Add Node (Property Bar)

Freehand: Pointer Tool (Select) then Pen Tool

This tool is used to add anchor points to paths e.g. you may need extra anchor points to edit or reshape a garment.

Exercise 7: *Add an anchor point to the bodice.*

Switching between tools is common - if a technique is not working check you are using the correct tool.

- **Illustrator:** Select the tool for adding anchor points
  - Click on the **Path** to add an anchor point
- **CorelDraw:** Select the Shape Tool, click on the bodice to select it, click on the **Path** where you wish to add a node, click on the Add Node (Property Bar) to add a node
- **Freehand:** Select the Pointer Tool and select the path, then select the Pen Tool and click on the **Path** to add a Point

All Packages
- Select the tool for selecting anchor points (see exercise 6)
- Click and 'drag' the new anchor point

centre front

centre front

8. deleting anchor points

Illustrator: Delete Anchor Point Tool

CorelDRAW: Shape Tool and Delete Node (Property Bar)

Freehand: Pointer Tool and Pen Tool

This tool is used to delete anchor points from paths e.g. you may need to remove an anchor point to edit or reshape the garment.

Exercise 8: *Delete an anchor point from the bodice.*

Illustrator:
- Select the tool for deleting anchor points
- Click on the anchor point you wish to delete
- **CorelDRAW:** Select the Shape Tool, select the bodice, click on the node you wish to delete, click on the Delete Node (Property Bar)
- **Freehand:** Select the Pointer Tool and select the path, then select the Pen Tool and click on the point to delete the point

All Packages
- The 'path' snaps back to form its original path

centre front

centre front

9. shaping lines/objects

Illustrator: Convert Anchor Point Tool

CorelDRAW: Shape Tool and Convert Line to Curve (Property Bar)

Freehand: Subselect Tool

This tool is used to edit the shape of a path (objects and lines) e.g. make curves, change smooth points to corner points and vice versa.

Exercise 9: *Draw a zig-zag-line and shape to make smooth curves.*

'Shaping' is a frequently used technique - it is worth practising to perfect it.

All Packages

- Select the Pen Tool
- Click and move the cursor to draw a zig-zag line
- **Note:** *Keep the path selected (see exercise 5)*

- **Illustrator:** Select the Convert Anchor Point tool
- Click on an anchor point and drag (direction handles appear), drag and move the handle(s) to make smooth curves
- **Note:** *Pull anchor points in the same direction you drew them or the lines will cross*

NO **X**

- **CorelDRAW:** Select the Shape Tool
- Click on a node, click the Convert Line to Curve (Property Bar) to display contol points, click and drag the points to make smooth curves

- **Freehand:** Select the Subselect Tool
- Click on a point, click and drag the handles to create smooth curves

10. shaping flats

Illustrator: Convert Anchor Point Tool

CorelDRAW: Shape Tool, Convert Line to Curve, and Reverse curve direction (Property Bar)

Freehand: Subselect Tool

This tool is used to shape flats e.g. necklines, armholes, sleeve heads, side seam hiplines, hems.

Exercise 10: *Select and curve the bodice neckline and armhole.*

- **Illustrator:** Select the tool to shape objects, click on anchor point **1** at the centre front neckline and drag handles to curve neckline
- Click on ancor point 4 to curve armhole
- **CorelDRAW:** Select the Shape Tool, click on the path, click node 1, click on Reverse Direction (Property Bar), click Convert Line to Curve, click and drag handles to curve neckline
- Click node 4, click Convert Line to Curve, and curve armhole

- **Freehand:** Select the Subselect Tool, click on the path, click on point 1 to select it, then click and drag handles to curve neckline
- Click on point 4 to select it, then click and drag handles to curve armhole

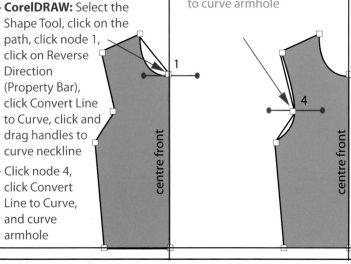

11. drawing circles and ovals (buttons)

Illustrator: Ellipse Tool

CorelDRAW: Ellipse Tool

Freehand: Ellipse Tool

This tool is used to draw circles and ovals e.g. excellent for drawing buttons and logos.

Exercise 11: *Create and align buttons on the centre front line of the bodice.*

All Packages
- Select the Ellipse Tool
- Hold down Shift, click and drag to make a circle(CorelDRAW hold down Ctrl) ●
- With the circle selected choose Edit (Menu Bar) >Copy, Edit>Paste (to create more buttons of equal size) ●
  ●
  ●
  ●
  ●

- Select the tool to select objects (see exercise 5)
- Select and drag a button to the top c/f neck point, and drag another to the bottom c/f point
- Drag the remaining buttons to position roughly between the top and bottom buttons
- Hold down Shift and select all the buttons

- **Illustrator:** Choose Window (Menu Bar)>Align (to display the Align palette), in the palette click Horizontal Align Center, then Vertical Distribute Center
- **CorelDRAW:** Arrange (Menu Bar)>Align and Distribute>Align and Distribute (to display the Align and Distribute box)
- Click Align tab>Center (left/right)
- Click Distribute tab>Center (Top/Bottom)
- Click Apply
- **Freehand:** Window (Menu) >Align (to display the Align panel), on the box next to the Horizontal buttons, click Distribute centers
- On the box next to the Vertical buttons, click Align center
- Click Apply

All Packages
- If necessary, hold down Shift, select the buttons and move them to the c/f line

c/f

12. drawing rectangles (pockets)

Illustrator: Rectangle Tool

CorelDRAW: Rectangle Tool

Freehand: Rectangle Tool

This tool is used to draw squares and rectangles e.g. excellent for drawing pockets, borders for presentations.

Exercise 12: *Draw a pocket and topstitching, group and position it on the bodice.*

When you group objects they behave as one, ungroup to treat them as individual objects.

All Packages
- Select the Rectangle Tool
- Click and drag to draw a rectangle

Topstitching
- Select the Pen Tool
- Click and draw a line just below the top edge of the pocket, select a dashed Stroke/line, (exercise 3b)
- Hold down 'Shift', and with the tool to select objects, select the dashed line and pocket
- **Illustrator:** Choose Object (Menu Bar)>Group
- **CorelDRAW:** Arrange (Menu Bar)>Group
- **Freehand:** Modify (Menu)>Group

- Select the tool to select objects, select the pocket, drag to position it on the bodice

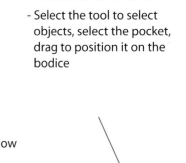

c/f

- *Note: For a square pocket, hold down Shift as you drag*

13. rotating objects

 Illustrator: Rotate Tool (or Object>Transform>Rotate)

CorelDRAW: Pick Tool, or Angle of Rotation (Property Bar) (or Windows>Dockers>Transformations>Rotate)

 Freehand: Rotate Tool [or Window>Object (to display the Object Panel), click the Add Effect icon>Transform]

This tool is used to rotate an object around a fixed point and position it to any angle required e.g. a garment or pocket. You can also add values by using the commands.

Exercise 13: *Rotate the pocket on the bodice.*

All Packages
- Select the tool to select objects and select the pocket
- Select the tool to rotate objects
- Click on one of the corner anchor points on the pocket and drag to rotate the pocket to desired angle
- **CorelDRAW:** Double click to display the Rotate icon, then drag to rotate

- **Freehand:** The further you move the Rotate Tool along the handle, the smaller the increments of rotation

- *Note: Use the commands and enter values for more precision*

14. creating text

Illustrator: Type Tool

CorelDRAW: Text Tool

Freehand: Text Tool

This tool is used to create and edit text e.g. particularly useful for technical instructions, for specification drawings, or for text on presentations

Exercise 14: *Create a logo on the pocket.*

All Packages
- Select the tool for creating text, click away from the bodice and type the letter 'T'
- Select tool to select objects, select the text
- **Illustrator:** Choose Window (Menu Bar)>Type (to display the Type palette)>Character and select the font and size
- **CorelDRAW:** Choose font size etc. from the Property Bar
- **Freehand:** Choose font size etc. from the Text Toolbar

- Select the tool to select objects, drag the text to the desired position on the garment

- Create text for specification instructions e.g.

Embroidered 'T' logo using red lurex thread

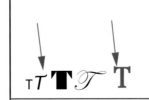

These 20 drawing tools and techniques can also be used to create dynamic fashion illustrations, fabric designs and presentations. Your scanned fashion illustrations, photographs and fabrics (see *Scanning and Digital Photography* chapter) can be brought into Illustrator, CorelDRAW or Freehand to enhance your presentations. Although, Photoshop tends to give more flexibility for editing and is often the preferred software for creating presentations when working with bitmap images.

This chapter has explained how to draw a basic bodice using 20 key drawing techniques. These basic skills form the foundation for the next chapter on drawing flats and specs where the techniques will be explained in more detail.

You can place/ import your flats (Vector images) and work between various graphics packages but the files must be saved in a suitable format, e.g. open Illustrator files in Photoshop and vice versa, save a CorelDraw file as an EPS and open it in Photoshop (see Chapter 3, Computer Basics).

You can resize your 'Vector' flats to any size (see Exercise 16).

As you master the techniques you will find there are several ways to create the same end results and will develop your preferred method of working.

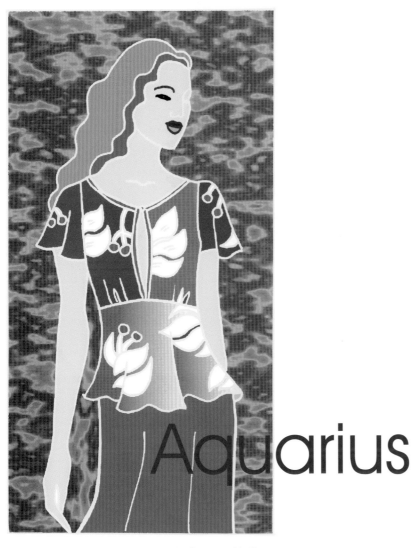

*Fashion Presentation by **Lynnette Cook,** created in Illustrator*

Live Trace (Illustrator), Corel PowerTRACE (CorelDRAW) and tracing software: *Tracing tools automatically trace an image. The only limitation is that you need to start with a clean template (a line drawing may be preferable) as every detail is traced. Textile designers find tracing tools especially useful to help create their prints.*

Tracing using the Pen Tool: *The figure in the illustration above was created using the Pen Tool. The illustrator took a digital photograph of a model (you could scan an image also), and in Illustrator, placed it on a layer and locked it, then created a new layer and traced over the image using the Pen tool. By zooming into the photograph she was able to accurately trace the model and create a vector drawing which she then edited (line, color and pattern).*

5

flats
and
specs
women

Fashion Illustration by **Stuart McKenzie**
Ink on paper, scanned illustration and
fabric swatch, edited in Photoshop

Fashion designers require a portfolio of computer drawing skills to sketch designs ranging from the simplest tank top through to the most highly styled creations. This includes drawing clothing as flats/working drawings, specification drawings (specs), and illustrated designs drawn on a fashion figure body/croquis.

This chapter demonstrates how to draw flats by applying the 20 key fashion drawing techniques using graphics drawing programmes; Illustrator, CorelDRAW and Freehand. These techniques were introduced in chapter 4, *Drawing Techniques,* and will be further developed to include the exercises and flats as presented in the table below.

The techniques described here apply to all drawing software.

exercises
1. Female Croquis (Figure Template)
2. Tank Top (Stretch Fabric)
3. Top with Sleeves and Style Variations
4. Fitted Shirt/Blouse and Style Variations
5. Fitted Skirt (Pencil) and Style Variations
6. Fitted Pant and Style Variations
7. Fitted Dress and Style Variations
8. Design Details - zips, pockets etc.
9. Specs (Specification Sheets)
10. Library of Styles

Table of flats exercises

flats / working drawings

Flats are explicit line drawings of garments, drawn to scale, using simple, clear lines, with no exaggeration of detail as you would find in a more stylized fashion illustration. All construction lines such as seams, darts, and styling details, such as pockets, buttons, and trims, are represented.

Fashion companies use flats as their primary visual source to communicate and liaise with buyers, clients, pattern makers and sample machinists - flats are the international fashion language. As part of the design process, digital drawings are the most efficient method to communicate designs from the fashion design studio to production, and to the buyers, merchandisers, and marketing teams.

As you work through this chapter and develop your computer drawing skills you will find that sketching flats on the computer is a quick and efficient method of drawing clothing.

Bra Top, created in Illustrator and filled with a gradient

A-line skirt with asymmetrical pleated wrap, created in CorelDRAW and 'Filled' with color and a Pattern

1. female croquis (figure template)

Fig. 5.1 is a female croquis/figure template and can be used as a guide to achieve the correct proportions when drawing flats. The croquis stands straight, balanced on both feet with shoulder and hips level, and with normal body proportions (approximately seven to eight head depths in height). The 'fit/style lines' on the body of the croquis are identical to those on a mannequin and are used to achieve the correct shape and fit when drafting patterns (see my book *'Fashion Artist'* on how to draw a croquis).

creating a figure template / croquis

1. To use the croquis, either scan them or take digital photographs and transfer the images to your computer, (see Chapter 8, *Scanning and Digital Photography*). You could also create your own croquis in Illustrator, CorelDRAW or Freehand by developing the techniques in Chapter 4, *Drawing Techniques*.
2. Create a folder called 'Croquis' and name the files accordingly e.g. female_front, female_back. Use this folder to store and retrieve your figure croquis for women, men, and children.

drawing flats

The following flats are created using the techniques covered in Chapter 4, *Drawing Techniques*. As you practise these techniques and become confident in using the tools you will find there are many ways to achieve similar results.

To get started:

1. Open your drawing program and create a new file
2. Choose File>Place (Import), and select the croquis
3. Name the file as per the style of garment e.g. tank_top, pencil_skirt
4. To prevent mistakenly drawing on the croquis layer you should lock the croquis layer or hide the drawing tool icon next to it
5. A 1 pt stroke line has been used for drawing the flats, a 0.75 pt stroke for the topstitching, and a 0.5 pt for finer details where appropriate.

Stylised mannequin - part of a presentation created from a digital photograph, scanned images and edited in Photoshop, created by Frances Howie

NOTE

The flats in these exercises have been filled with colour to make them easier to read. In the fashion industry, flats are often presented as black and white 'line art' and shaded where necessary, and created in color for presentation work.

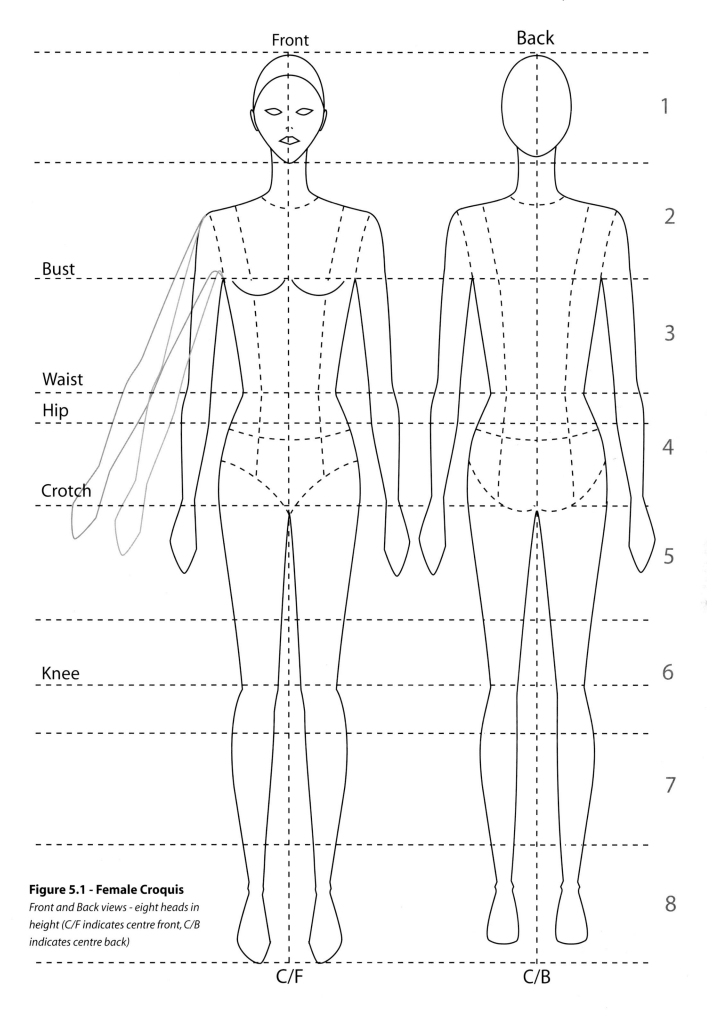

Front   Back

Bust

Waist

Hip

Crotch

Knee

1

2

3

4

5

6

7

8

C/F   C/B

Figure 5.1 - Female Croquis
*Front and Back views - eight heads in
height (C/F indicates centre front, C/B
indicates centre back)*

2. tank top (stretch fabric)

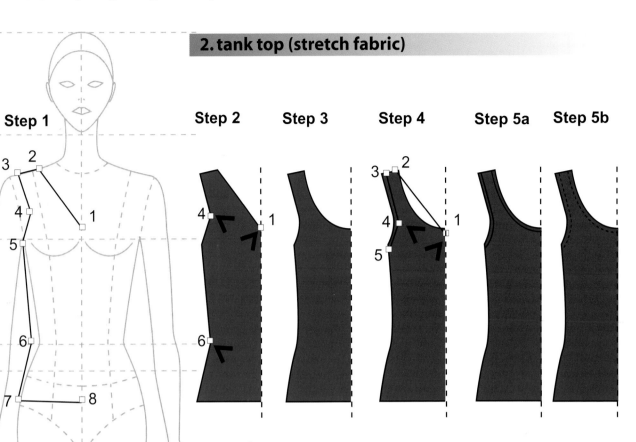

Step 1   **Step 2**   **Step 3**   **Step 4**   **Step 5a**   **Step 5b**

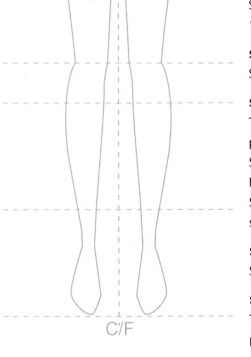

step 1

Select the Pen Tool, place the first anchor point **1** on the C/F lower neck point, then create anchor points **2** to **8**. (Illustrator: Make sure the color 'Fill' is on).

step 2

Select the tool for shaping, and drag the handles to shape:
1 curve neckline, **4** curve armhole, **6** smooth waist to hip line.

step 3

Shows curved neckline, curved armhole and smooth waist to hip line.

step 4

To draw a bound neckline and bound armhole place additional anchor points a fraction in from the edges:
Select the Pen Tool and make anchor points **1** and finish at **2**.
In addition make anchor points **3**, **4** and finish at **5**.
Select the tool for shaping objects and drag the handles to follow the shape of the original neckline and armhole.

step 5a

Shows bound neck and bound armhole.

step 5b

Topstitching - Select the bound neck and armhole lines and make them a 2 pt dash.

Figure 5.2
Tank top (stretch fabric - darts are not required)

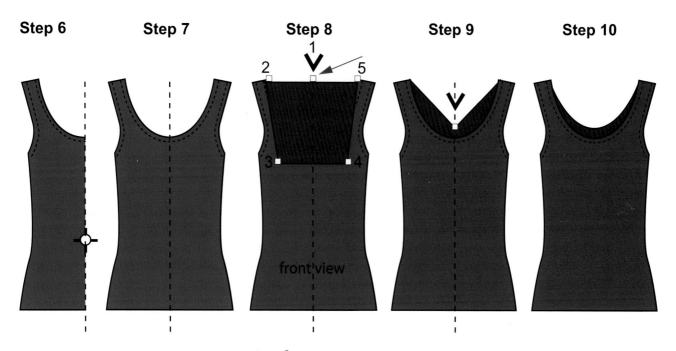

step 6

Select the tool for selecting objects, select all, and group (*Drawing Techniques* chapter, exercise 12).

Use the technique for Reflecting (*Drawing Techniques* chapter, exercise 17).

step 7

Shows both sides of tank top (symmetrical).

('Fill' if required - *Drawing Techniques* chapter, exercise 18).

step 8

Back neck view - select the Pen Tool, place anchor point *1* on the C/F line, then create anchor points *2* to *5,* and finish back at *1* (close path).

Select the back neck shape and 'Fill' with a darker tone.

Select the back neck shape and 'Send to Back' (*Drawing Techniques* chapter, exercise 19).

step 9

Select the tool to move anchor points, drag point *1* down to finish above front neckline.

Select the tool for shaping, drag the handles to make a smooth 'back neck'.

step 10

Shows the completed tank top front including shape of the back neck.

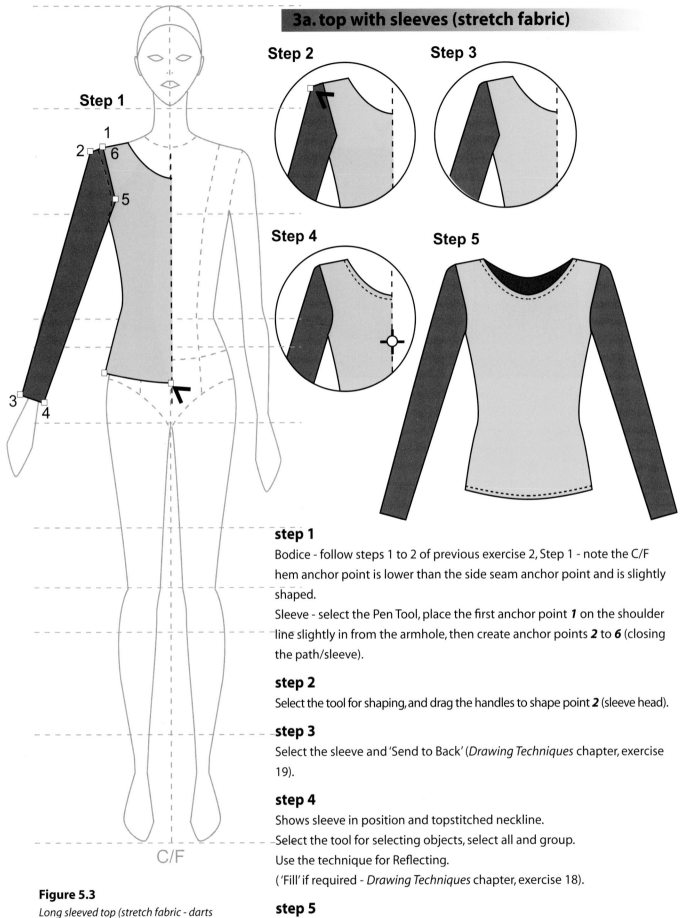

3a. top with sleeves (stretch fabric)

Step 1

Step 2

Step 3

Step 4

Step 5

Figure 5.3
Long sleeved top (stretch fabric - darts are not required)

step 1
Bodice - follow steps 1 to 2 of previous exercise 2, Step 1 - note the C/F hem anchor point is lower than the side seam anchor point and is slightly shaped.

Sleeve - select the Pen Tool, place the first anchor point *1* on the shoulder line slightly in from the armhole, then create anchor points *2* to *6* (closing the path/sleeve).

step 2
Select the tool for shaping, and drag the handles to shape point *2* (sleeve head).

step 3
Select the sleeve and 'Send to Back' (*Drawing Techniques* chapter, exercise 19).

step 4
Shows sleeve in position and topstitched neckline.
Select the tool for selecting objects, select all and group.
Use the technique for Reflecting.
('Fill' if required - *Drawing Techniques* chapter, exercise 18).

step 5
Back neck - use the technique from the previous tank top exercise 2, Steps 8 and 9.
Shows the completed basic top with sleeves.

3b. top variation - 'V' neck

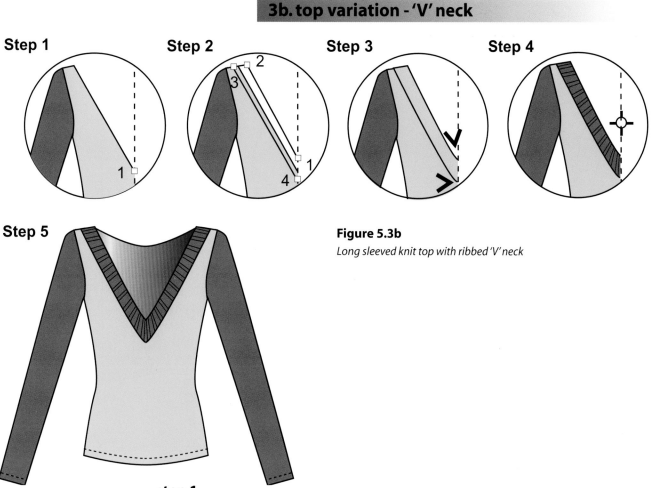

Step 1 **Step 2** **Step 3** **Step 4**

Step 5

Figure 5.3b
Long sleeved knit top with ribbed 'V' neck

step 1
Follow steps 1 to 3 of previous exercise 3a, but place the C/F neck point *1* lower for this 'V' neck style.

step 2
Neck Band - select the Pen Tool and create anchor points *1* to *4*.

step 3
Select the tool for shaping, drag the handles to shape points *1* and *4* (when reflected the 'V' point will be less severe).

step 4
Rib neckline - select the Pen Tool and create individual lines - position and rotate these lines slightly to make sure they fit within the neck band. Here the lines have been grouped in pairs to indicate a 2x2 rib.

step 5
Select the tool for selecting objects, select all and group.
Use the technique for 'Reflecting'.
Bodice and sleeve hem - select the Pen Tool and create 2 pt dashed stroke lines, allowing a deeper space between the stitching and the hem (this indicates a covered hem, a popular finish for stretch garments).
('Fill' if required - *Drawing Techniques* chapter, exercise 18).
Back neck - use the technique from the previous tank top exercise 2, Steps 8 and 9 - but for this exercise fill the back neck shape with a gradient (*Drawing Techniques* chapter, exercise 20).
Shows the completed basic top with sleeves.

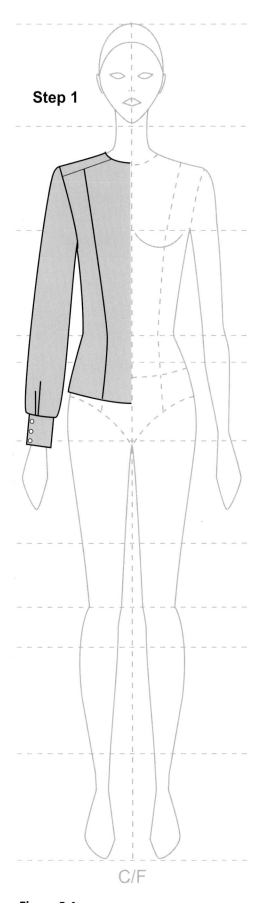

Step 1

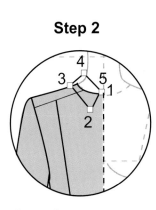

Step 2

4a. fitted shirt

Step 4

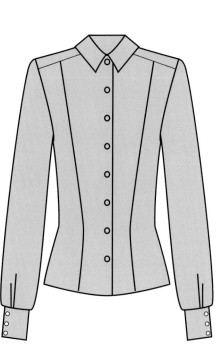

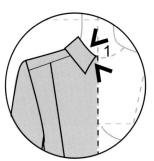

Step 3

C/F

Figure 5.4
Fitted shirt with collar, deep cuffs and button front

step 1
Select the Pen Tool and draw the left half of the shirt, the side front fit line, and front shoulder yoke.
Shape the neck, armhole, side seam, and front hem.
Draw the sleeve (cuff, tuck lines and buttons) and 'send to back'.

step 2
Collar - Select the Pen Tool, place anchor point **1** just above the C/F neck, then create point **2** collar tip, point **3** on shoulder line, point **4** touching the neck, and point **5** (to close collar / path).

step 3
Select the tool for shaping, and drag handles to shape a slight curve on the collar's neck and front edges.
Use the technique for 'Reflecting'.
('Fill' if required - refer *Drawing Techniques* chapter exercise 18).

step 4
Back neck - use the technique from the basic tank top exercise 2, Steps 8 and 9.
Buttons - refer *Basic Drawing Techniques* chapter 4, exercise 11. Note the buttons must line up centrally on the centre front line.
Button wrap / Extension - Select the Pen Tool and draw a line to form the button wrap / extension.
Shows the completed shirt.

4b. top

Printed cowl neckline top with
detachable soft leather flower brooch,
created in CorelDRAW by Linda Logan

4c. lingerie style top

Camisole top with bra style front cups,
decorative tucks and decorative stitching
on body, spaghetti straps, created in
CorelDRAW by Linda Logan

4d. swimsuit

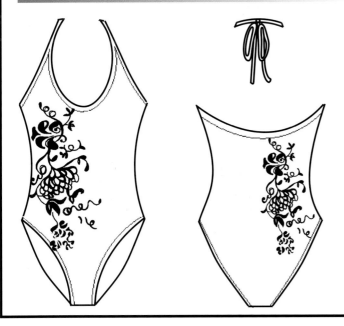

Tie halter neck costume with front and
back pattern detail, created in Illustrator
by Lynnette Cook

4e. shirt (front)

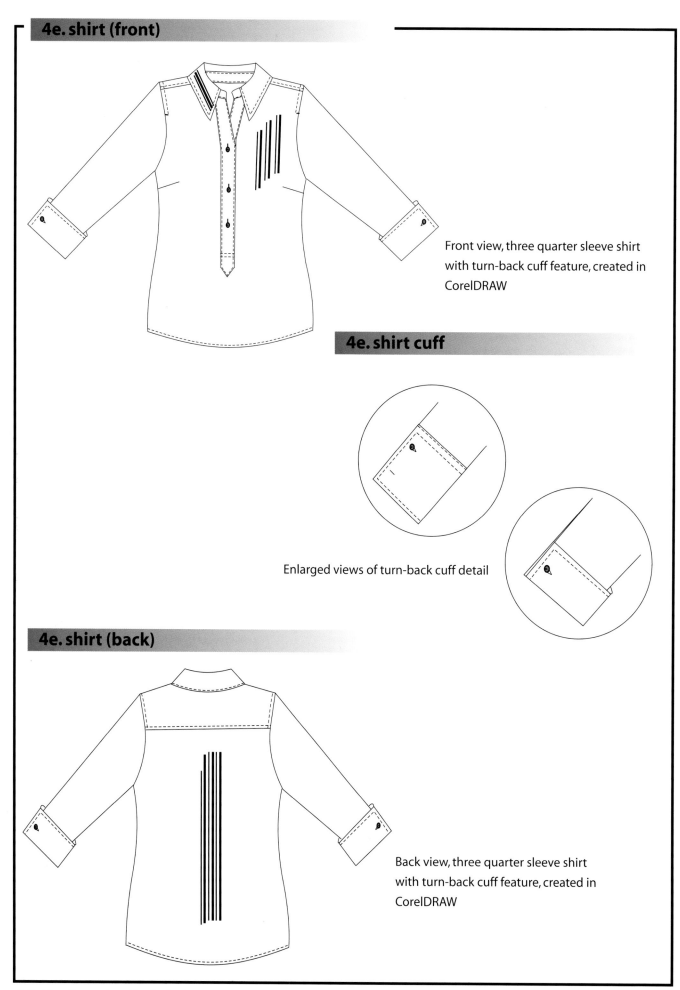

Front view, three quarter sleeve shirt with turn-back cuff feature, created in CorelDRAW

4e. shirt cuff

Enlarged views of turn-back cuff detail

4e. shirt (back)

Back view, three quarter sleeve shirt with turn-back cuff feature, created in CorelDRAW

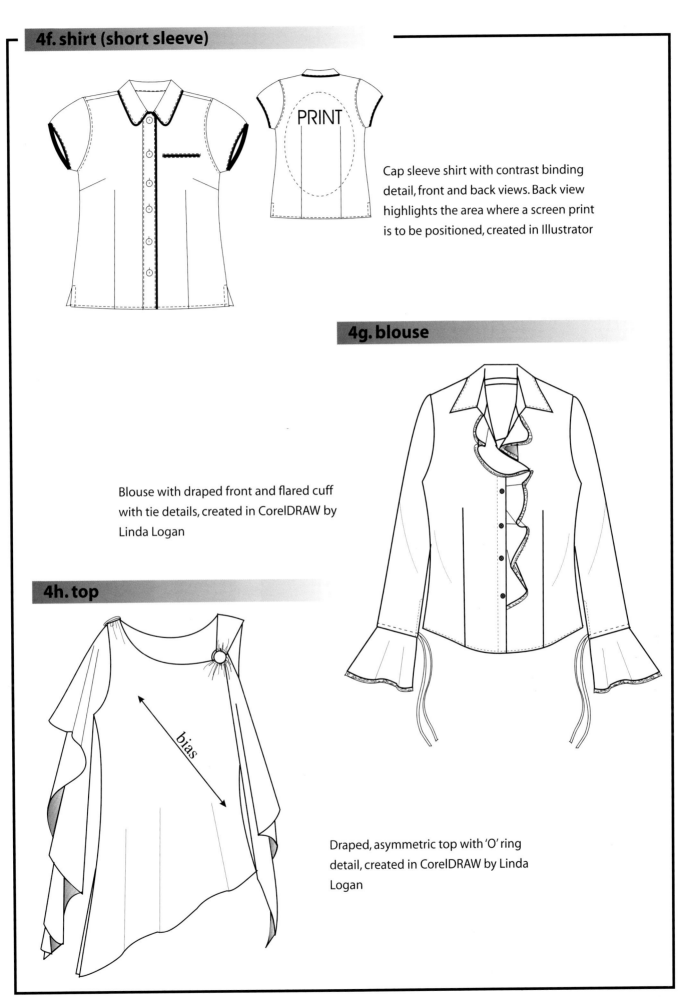

4f. shirt (short sleeve)

PRINT

Cap sleeve shirt with contrast binding detail, front and back views. Back view highlights the area where a screen print is to be positioned, created in Illustrator

4g. blouse

Blouse with draped front and flared cuff with tie details, created in CorelDRAW by Linda Logan

4h. top

bias

Draped, asymmetric top with 'O' ring detail, created in CorelDRAW by Linda Logan

5e. A-line skirt

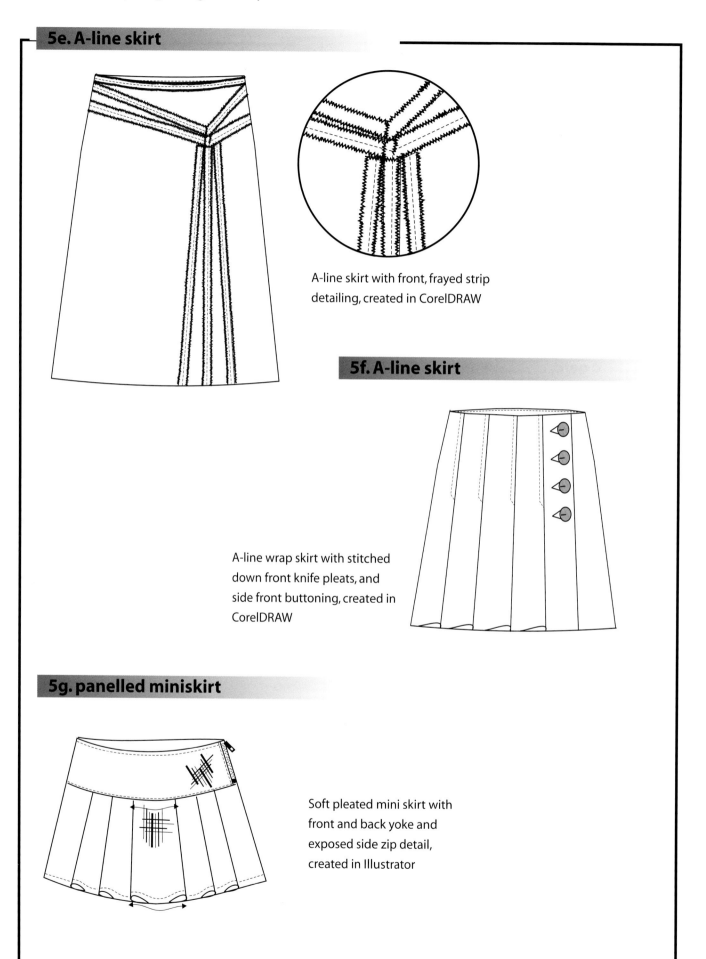

A-line skirt with front, frayed strip detailing, created in CorelDRAW

5f. A-line skirt

A-line wrap skirt with stitched down front knife pleats, and side front buttoning, created in CorelDRAW

5g. panelled miniskirt

Soft pleated mini skirt with front and back yoke and exposed side zip detail, created in Illustrator

5h. panelled skirt

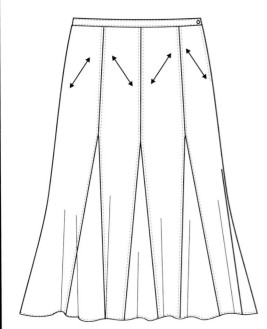

Bias cut panelled skirt with insets to create flare and fullness from the hip, created in CorelDRAW by Linda Logan

5i. bias cut skirt

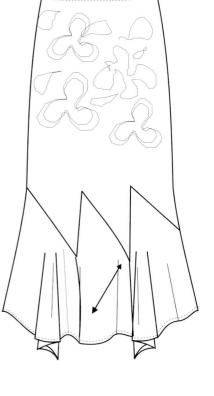

Bias cut skirt with bias cut asymmetric inserts front and back creating fullness and an irregular hemline, created in CorelDRAW by Linda Logan

5j. A-line skirt

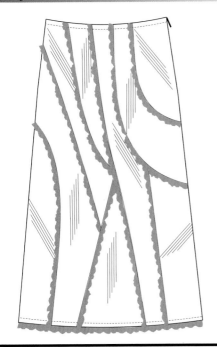

INDICATES PINSTRIPE DIRECTION

Pinstripe fabric A-line skirt with front and back tulle trim decorative detailing, created in Illustrator

6a. fitted pant

step 1

Select the Pen Tool and place anchor point *1* on the C/F waistline, create anchor points *2* to *7*, and create the front dart.

step 2

Select the tool for shaping, drag handles to shape point *3* to create a smooth hip.

step 3

Waistband - select the Pen Tool place anchor point *1* above the waistline on the C/F line, then create anchor points *2* to *4*

step 4

Select and drag the waistband to fit on top of the pant waistline.
Use the technique for 'Reflecting'.

step 5

Centre front line and zip - select the Pen Tool and create anchor points *1* to *2*; create a 2 pt dashed line of 0.75 pt to indicate the front zip.
Select the Ellipse Tool and create the button.
('Fill' if required - refer *Drawing Techniques* chapter, exercise 18).
Shows the completed pant.

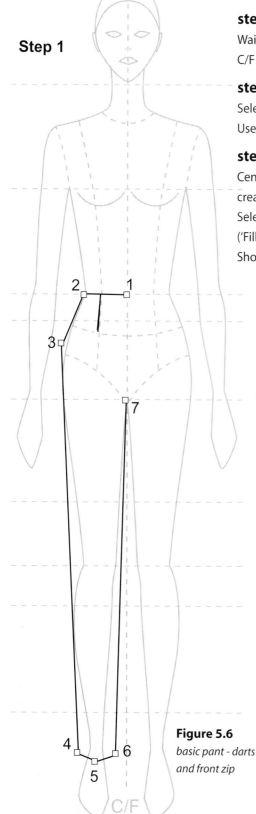

Step 1

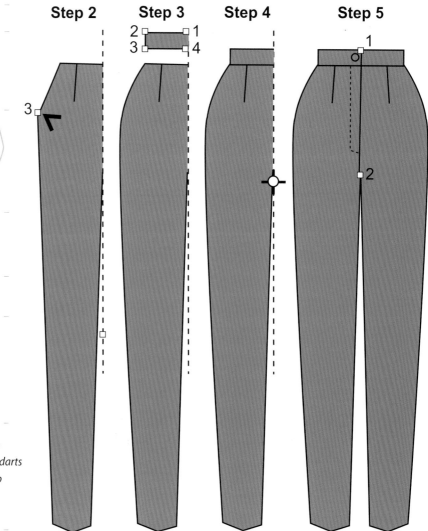

Figure 5.6
basic pant - darts and front zip

6b. flat front pant

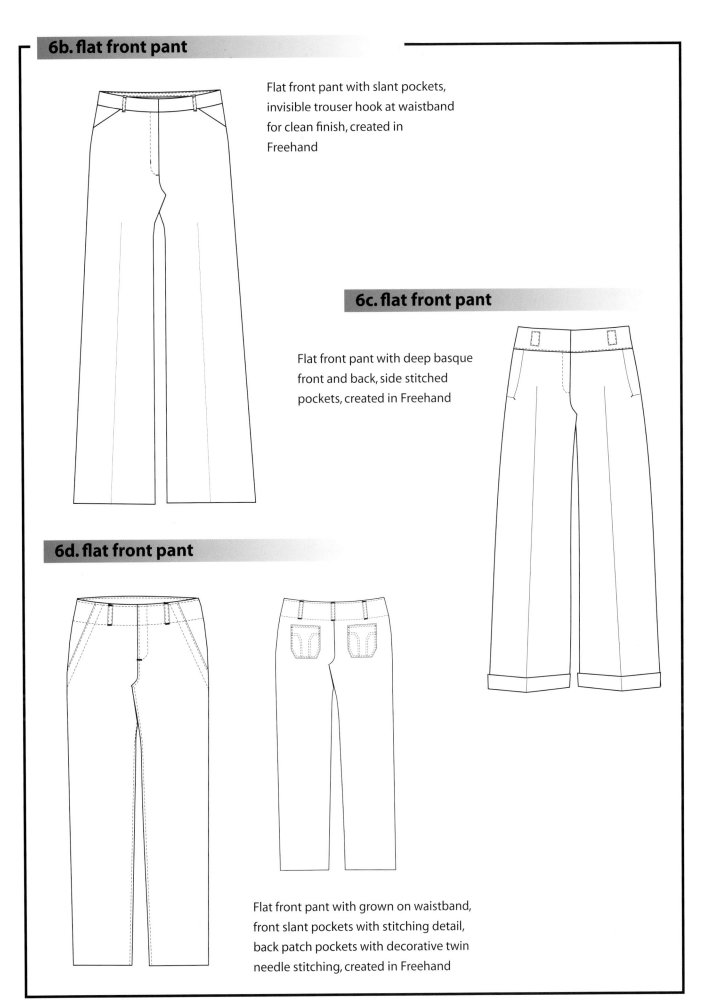

Flat front pant with slant pockets,
invisible trouser hook at waistband
for clean finish, created in
Freehand

6c. flat front pant

Flat front pant with deep basque
front and back, side stitched
pockets, created in Freehand

6d. flat front pant

Flat front pant with grown on waistband,
front slant pockets with stitching detail,
back patch pockets with decorative twin
needle stitching, created in Freehand

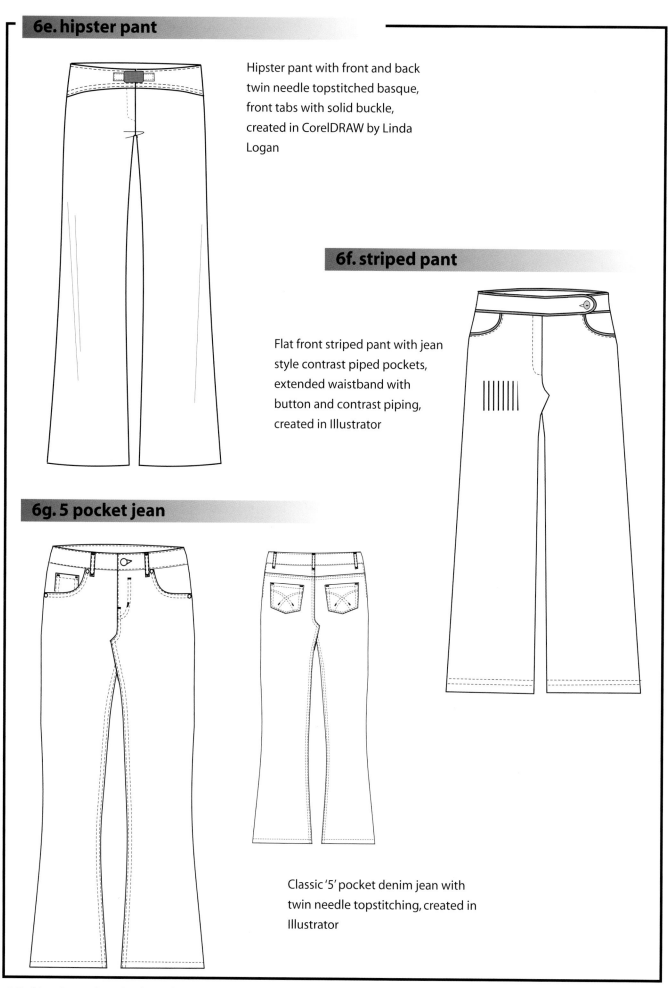

6e. hipster pant

Hipster pant with front and back twin needle topstitched basque, front tabs with solid buckle, created in CorelDRAW by Linda Logan

6f. striped pant

Flat front striped pant with jean style contrast piped pockets, extended waistband with button and contrast piping, created in Illustrator

6g. 5 pocket jean

Classic '5' pocket denim jean with twin needle topstitching, created in Illustrator

6h. pedal pushers/bermudas

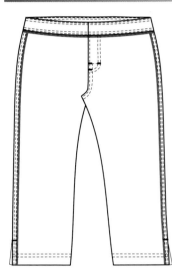 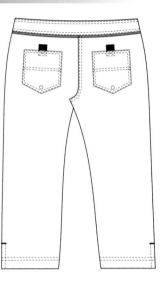

Pedal pushers/bermudas with side slits and contrast piping detail, back patch pockets with velcro tabs, studs/poppers and decorative twin needle topstitching, created in Freehand

6h. pedal pushers details

Highlighted details for pedal pushers/bermudas - patch pocket with twin needle topstitching, velcro tab

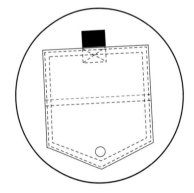

6i. flat front cropped pant

Flat front cropped pant with slant front pockets, tie belt, side slits with buttons, created in CorelDRAW by Linda Logan

7a. fitted dress

Step 1

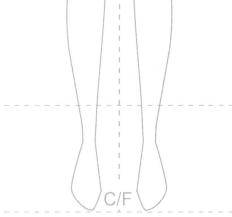

Step 2   **Step 3**   **Step 4**

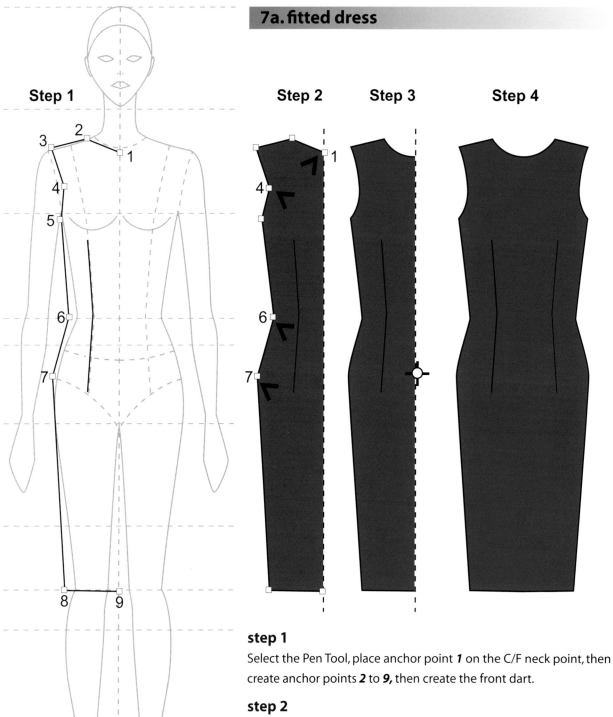

step 1

Select the Pen Tool, place anchor point **1** on the C/F neck point, then create anchor points **2** to **9,** then create the front dart.

step 2

Select the tool for shaping, and drag the handles to shape:
1 curve neckline, **4** curve armhole, **6** and **7** smooth waist to hip line.

step 3

Use the technique for 'Reflecting'.

step 4

('Fill' if required - refer *Drawing Techniques* chapter, exercise 18).

Shows the completed basic fitted dress.

Figure 5.7
Fitted dress with darts

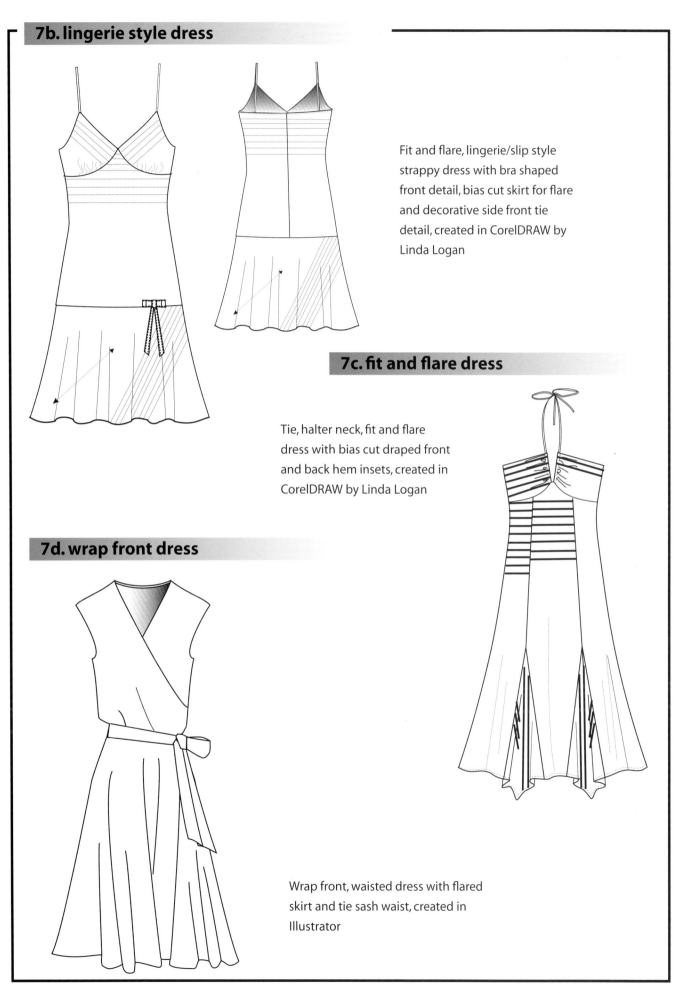

7b. lingerie style dress

Fit and flare, lingerie/slip style
strappy dress with bra shaped
front detail, bias cut skirt for flare
and decorative side front tie
detail, created in CorelDRAW by
Linda Logan

7c. fit and flare dress

Tie, halter neck, fit and flare
dress with bias cut draped front
and back hem insets, created in
CorelDRAW by Linda Logan

7d. wrap front dress

Wrap front, waisted dress with flared
skirt and tie sash waist, created in
Illustrator

8a. drape and cowl necklines

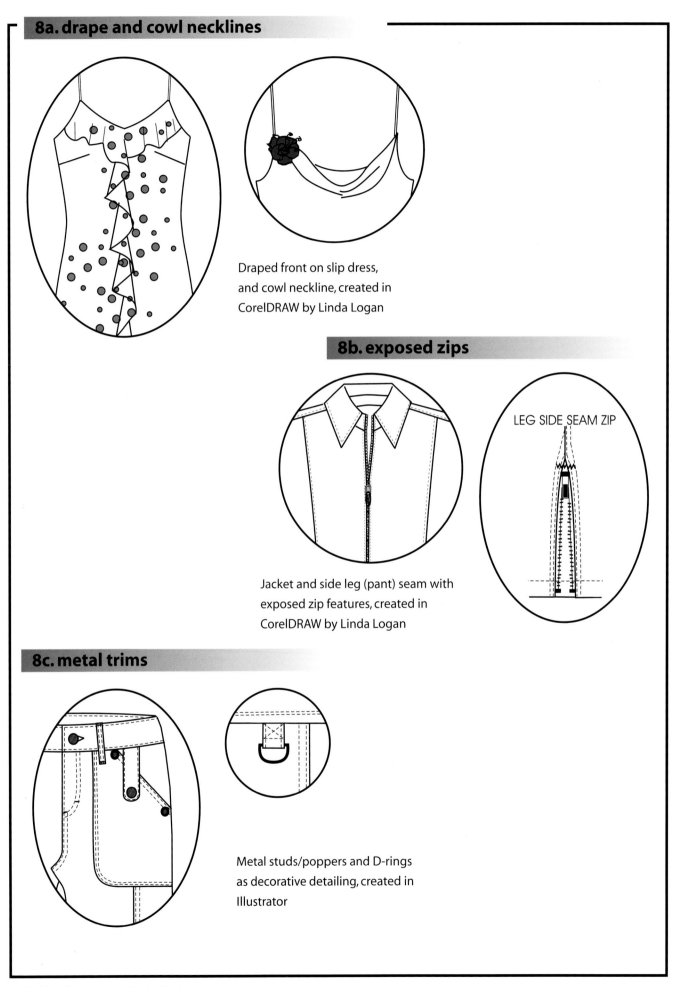

Draped front on slip dress,
and cowl neckline, created in
CorelDRAW by Linda Logan

8b. exposed zips

LEG SIDE SEAM ZIP

Jacket and side leg (pant) seam with
exposed zip features, created in
CorelDRAW by Linda Logan

8c. metal trims

Metal studs/poppers and D-rings
as decorative detailing, created in
Illustrator

8d. drawstrings

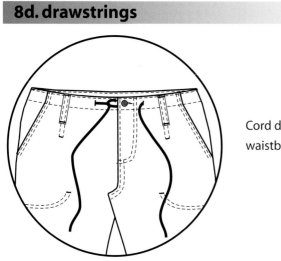

Cord drawstrings and loop on pant waistband, created in Freehand

8e. belts, tabs and pockets

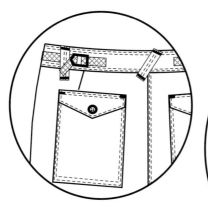

Twin needle topstitched belt loops, and pockets, webbing tabs, and belt with metal buckle, created in Freehand

8f. pockets

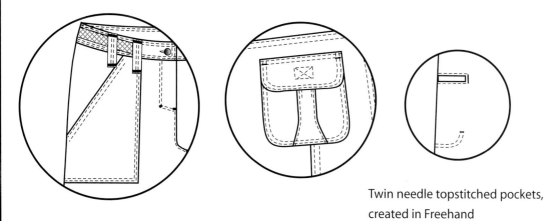

Twin needle topstitched pockets, created in Freehand

9. specs (specification sheets)

A spec sheet (specification sheet) is a document that contains an accurately drawn flat, and specifications (instructions and measurements). This information is needed to produce garments to the required standard and design. It forms the basis of a binding contract between the design house or client, and the factory that produces the garment. With a large percentage of clothing manufacturing being outsourced offshore, this document must be clear, precise and self explanatory.

Spec sheets can contain the following details (see Figure 6.8, and 6.9):
- a technical drawing(s) to show the exact design and details such as the position of pockets, buttons, labels
- measurements of the sample garment, plus graded sizes
- specific construction details such as the types of seams required, hem and topstitching details
- fabric details, a swatch of the fabric, and details of the trims and thread

The spec sheet can be adapted for various uses, for example:
- in the sample room where the pattern and sample garment is made
- the production area where the garment will be costed, and the factory floor where the garment orders are cut and constructed
- it may also be adapted and used in the despatching and delivery of the garments.

spec sheet document

Finished Flat Measurements - size Medium
1. Total Length................
2. Chest Circumference..............
3. Hem Circumference................
4. Neck Width.............
Etc................
Stitching: **Single Needle:** C.F. Zipper Edges, Raglan Seams, Hood Panels;   **Twin Needle:** Hem, Sleeve Cuff, Pocket Bag Stitching
Labelling: **Sew In Label** - Woven Label for Sizes S-L, position...........   **Care Label -** As Per Garment Instructions
Accessories: **Zip Slider:** To Be Reversible Same Style as Per Original Sample   **Drawcord:** Hood as Per Original Sample   **Velcro:** 2cm Wide Velcro For CF
Fabric: **Shell:** 100% Nylon Taslon   **Lining:** 100% Polyester Anti Pill Spun Polar Fleece - 280GM/M2   **Color Combinations:** Stone, Mink, Black with Contrast Lining

Fig. 6.8
Spec Sheet document showing an extract of the style details

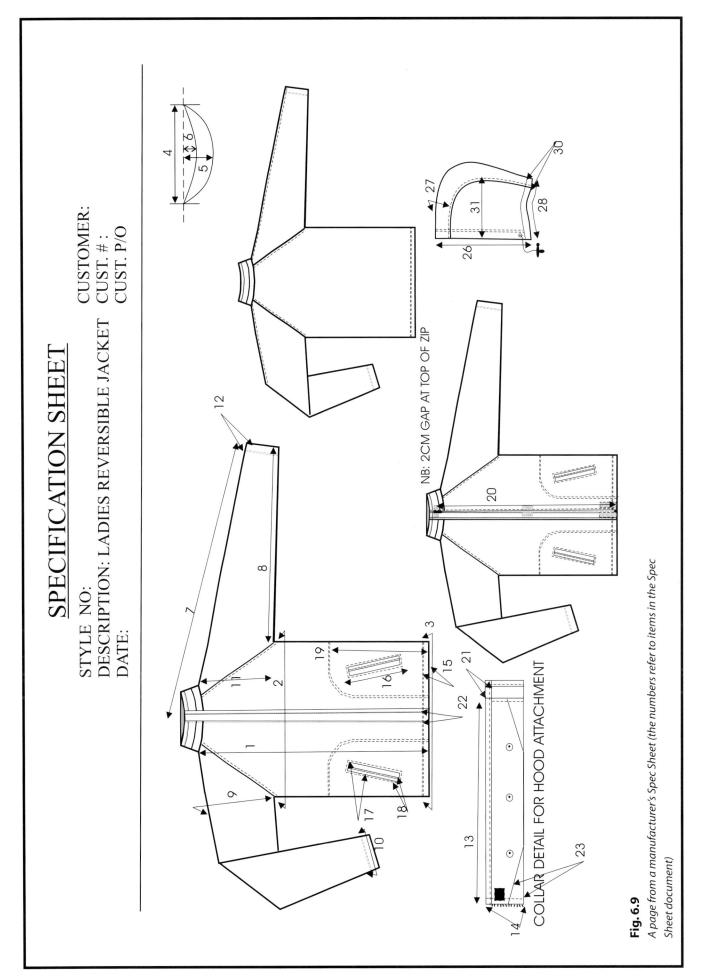

SPECIFICATION SHEET

CUSTOMER:

STYLE NO:
DESCRIPTION: LADIES REVERSIBLE JACKET
DATE:

CUST. # :
CUST. P/O

NB: 2CM GAP AT TOP OF ZIP

COLLAR DETAIL FOR HOOD ATTACHMENT

Fig. 6.9

A page from a manufacturer's Spec Sheet (the numbers refer to items in the Spec Sheet document)

STRETCH PERFORMANCE SERIES

STYLE: ANGEL SHIRT

WOMENS LONG SLEEVE SHIRT
FABRIC: MTS-MID
SIZES: S - XL
WHOLESALE $
SUGGESTED RETAIL $

COLOURS	S	M	L	XL	TOTAL
STORMY BLUE					
BLACK					

STYLE: ALL ABOUT EVE

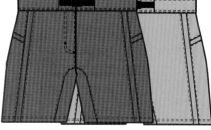

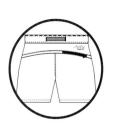

WOMENS SHORT SHORT
FABRIC: MTS-MID
SIZES: S - XL
WHOLESALE $
SUGGESTED RETAIL $

COLOURS	S	M	L	XL	TOTAL
SLATE					
STORMY BLUE					

STYLE: FLAMINGO ROAD

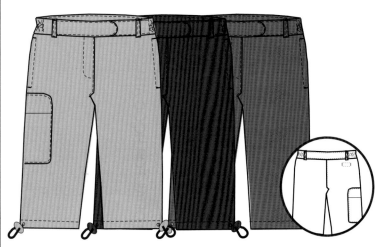

WOMENS 3/4 SHORT
FABRIC: MTS-MID
SIZES: S - XL
WHOLESALE $
SUGGESTED RETAIL $

COLOURS	S	M	L	XL	TOTAL
LIGHT TAUPE					
OLIVE					
SLATE					

Fig. 6.10
Presentation of flats for retail listing colors, sizes, cost etc.

10. library of styles

As you develop your computer drawing skills, you will find it useful to develop your own digital 'fashion library' of clothing shapes and style details.

Fashion libraries are excellent for retrieving files such as dress shapes, skirt shapes, various collars, cuffs etc. Digital libraries are particularly important for fashion designers because, as their portfolio of digital designs develops they will spend less time drawing from scratch and more time manipulating and adapting existing designs.

For example, a buyer might order several styles from your collection but, in addition, require a pencil skirt which is not in your collection. This style can be retrieved immediately from your library of styles, skirts folder, and the image sketched, and presented to the buyer.

More examples and their style descriptions can be found in my book *Fashion Design - Catwalk to Street.*

You can place/ import your flats (Vector images) and work between various graphics packages but the files must be saved in a suitable format, e.g. open Illustrator files in Photoshop and vice versa, save a CorelDraw file as an EPS and open it in Photoshop (see Chapter 3, Computer Basics).

You can resize your 'Vector' flats to any size (see Chapter 4, Drawing Techniques, exercise 16).

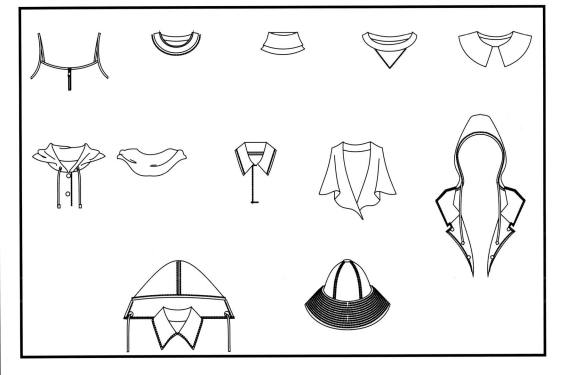

Fig. 6.11
*Library of necklines, collars and headgear courtesy of **Lectra Pty Ltd., NZ** and **SnapFashun Inc**.*

This chapter has explained how to draw several basic clothing styles for womenswear by using the skills learnt in Chapter 4, *Drawing Techniques.* These skills form the foundation for the following chapters on drawing flats for men and children, and for creating fashion presentations.

*An **instructor's manual** with additional exercises will be available for lecturers, see www.knowledgezone.net*

6

menswear

Fashion Illustration by **Alissa Stytsenko-Berdnik**
Ink on paper, scanned illustration and fabric swatch, edited in Illustrator and Photoshop

Menswear silhouettes change very little from season to season compared to womenswear silhouettes. The styling is created, primarily, through fabric, color and style details.

This chapter demonstrates how to draw flats for menswear by applying the 20 key fashion drawing techniques using graphics drawing programs Illustrator, CorelDRAW and Freehand. These techniques were introduced in the *Drawing Techniques* chapter 4, developed in *Flats and Specs,* chapter 5 and, in this chapter, will be further developed focusing on menswear (see table below).

exercises
1. Male Croquis (Figure Template)
2. Single Breasted Jacket
3. Casual Jackets
4. Shirts
5. Pants and Shorts

Table of menswear exercises

Fig. 6.1 is a male croquis/figure template and can be used as a guide to achieve the correct proportions when drawing flats. The croquis stands straight, balanced on both feet with shoulder and hips level, with normal body proportions (approximately seven to eight head depths in height).

menswear styling

When drawing flats for menswear there are several points to consider:
- Males are broader in frame compared to women, therefore garments are less fitted and defined e.g. no bust/chest darts, the waistline is similar in measurement to the hipline
- Jackets, shirts and pants fasten left over right

For more information, see my book *Fashion Artist.*

1. male croquis (figure template)

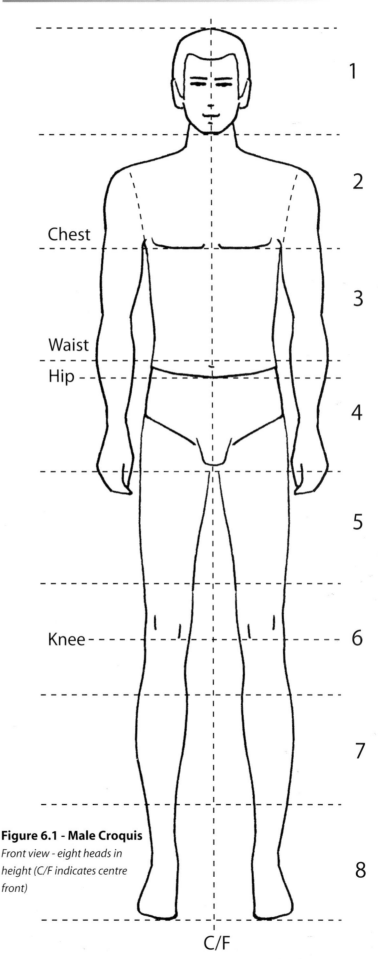

Figure 6.1 - Male Croquis
Front view - eight heads in height (C/F indicates centre front)

2. single breasted jacket

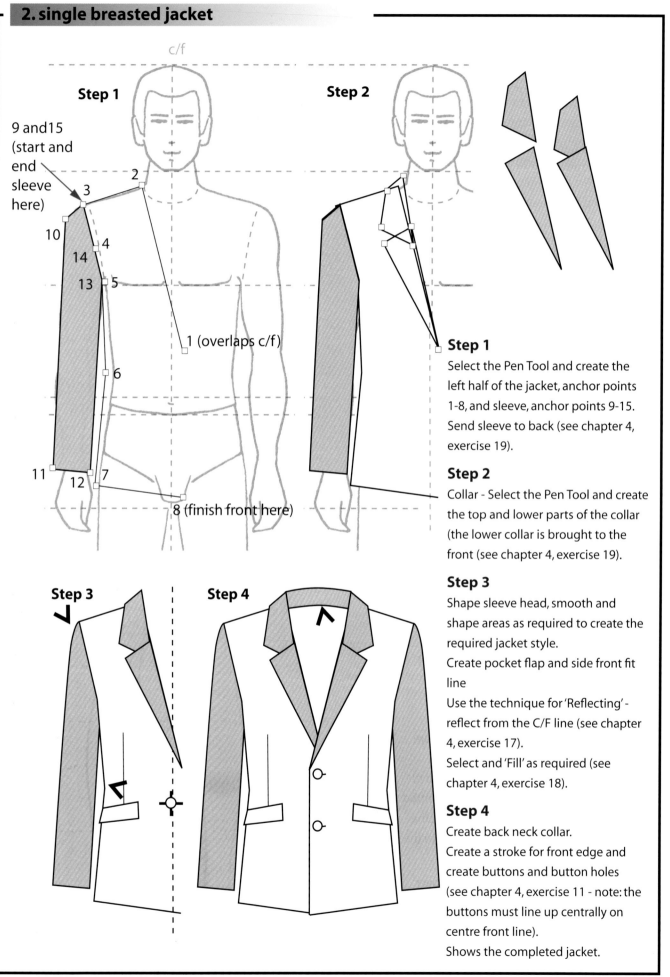

Step 1

9 and15 (start and end sleeve here)

2
3
10
4
14
13   5
1 (overlaps c/f)
6
11   7
12
8 (finish front here)

Step 2

Step 3

Step 4

Step 1

Select the Pen Tool and create the left half of the jacket, anchor points 1-8, and sleeve, anchor points 9-15. Send sleeve to back (see chapter 4, exercise 19).

Step 2

Collar - Select the Pen Tool and create the top and lower parts of the collar (the lower collar is brought to the front (see chapter 4, exercise 19).

Step 3

Shape sleeve head, smooth and shape areas as required to create the required jacket style.
Create pocket flap and side front fit line
Use the technique for 'Reflecting' - reflect from the C/F line (see chapter 4, exercise 17).
Select and 'Fill' as required (see chapter 4, exercise 18).

Step 4

Create back neck collar.
Create a stroke for front edge and create buttons and button holes (see chapter 4, exercise 11 - note: the buttons must line up centrally on centre front line).
Shows the completed jacket.

3a. nylon shell jacket

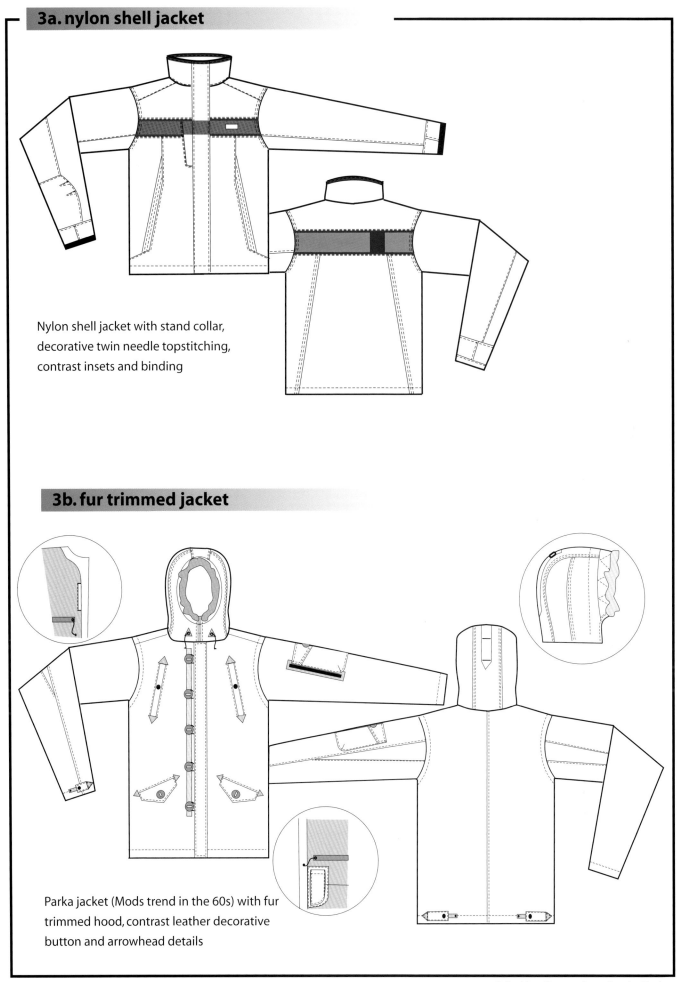

Nylon shell jacket with stand collar,
decorative twin needle topstitching,
contrast insets and binding

3b. fur trimmed jacket

Parka jacket (Mods trend in the 60s) with fur
trimmed hood, contrast leather decorative
button and arrowhead details

4a. long sleeve classic shirt

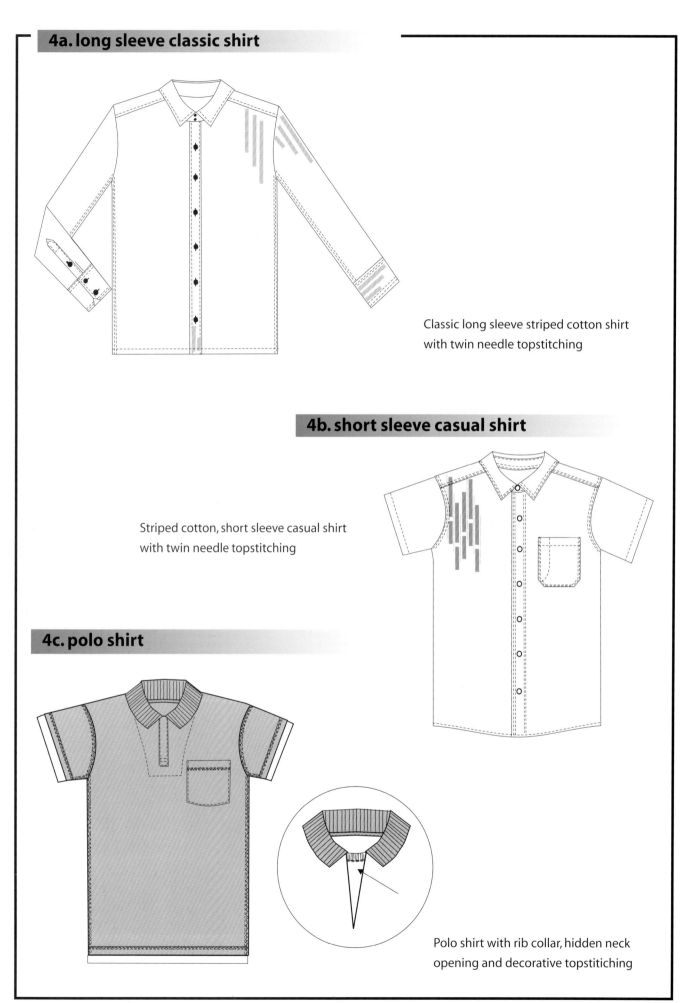

Classic long sleeve striped cotton shirt with twin needle topstitching

4b. short sleeve casual shirt

Striped cotton, short sleeve casual shirt with twin needle topstitching

4c. polo shirt

Polo shirt with rib collar, hidden neck opening and decorative topstitiching

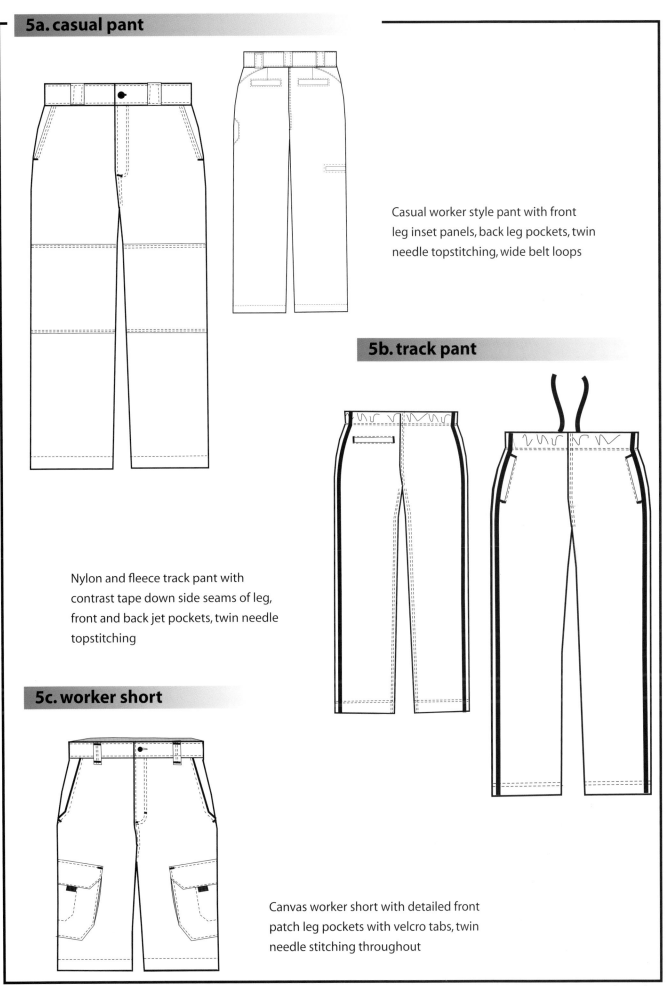

5a. casual pant

Casual worker style pant with front
leg inset panels, back leg pockets, twin
needle topstitching, wide belt loops

5b. track pant

Nylon and fleece track pant with
contrast tape down side seams of leg,
front and back jet pockets, twin needle
topstitching

5c. worker short

Canvas worker short with detailed front
patch leg pockets with velcro tabs, twin
needle stitching throughout

childrenswear

Pumpkin Patch®
EST. 1990
kid culture

Fashion Illustration by **Lynnette Cook**
Illustration hand drawn and edited in CorelDRAW

7

This chapter demonstrates how to draw flats for childrenswear by applying the 20 key drawing techniques using graphics drawing programmes; Illustrator, CorelDRAW and Freehand. These techniques were introduced in the *Drawing Techniques* chapter 4, developed in the previous chapters *Flats and Specs Women*, and *Menswear* and, in this chapter, will be further developed focusing on childrenswear (see table).

flats
1. Childrenswear Presentation
2. Babies Rompers and Dungarees
3. Kids Swims
4. Kids Bodysuits and Jackets
5. Dresses
6. Skirts
7. Tops, Shirts and Blouses

Table of childrenswear flats

Croquis for children, from an infant to young teen, can be found in the chapter on 'Children' in Fashion Artist.

1. childrenswear presentation

Designing childrenswear presents fashion designers with an interesting but fun challenge. The designer must be aware of the radically different sizes and special requirements of children from new borns to young teens. Styles include the more practical clothing that a baby wears, such as, bodysuits and rompers, more traditional designs such as 'pretty pink dresses', to the more fashionable styling following the trends of adult clothing and particularly influenced by young trendy pop stars.

*Fashion presentation by **Lynnette Cook***
Illustration hand drawn and edited in CorelDRAW

2. babies rompers and dungarees

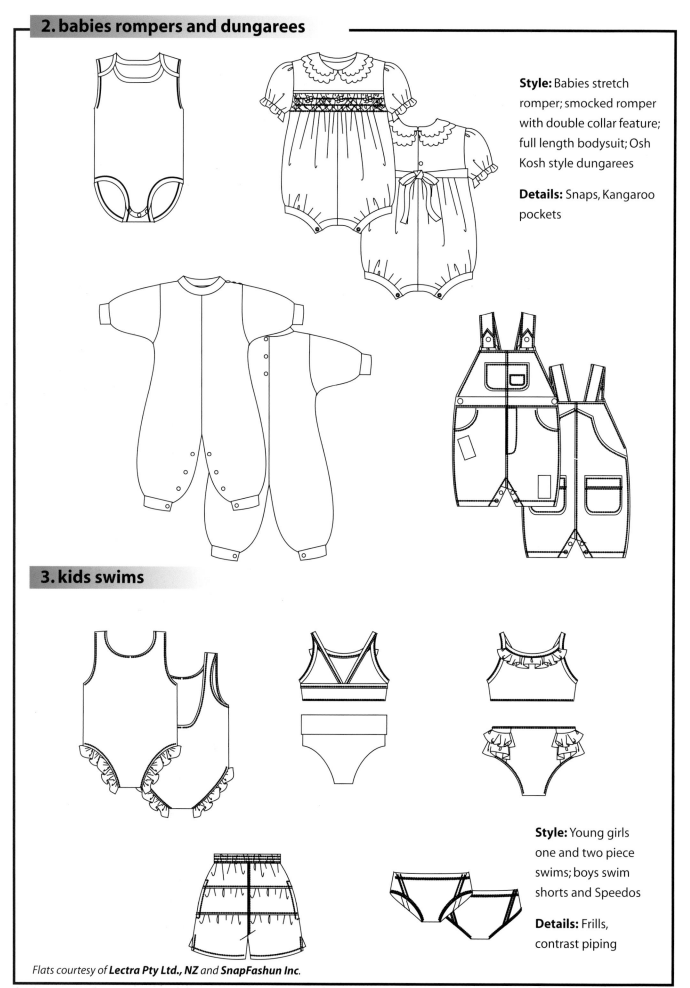

Style: Babies stretch romper; smocked romper with double collar feature; full length bodysuit; Osh Kosh style dungarees

Details: Snaps, Kangaroo pockets

3. kids swims

Style: Young girls one and two piece swims; boys swim shorts and Speedos

Details: Frills, contrast piping

*Flats courtesy of **Lectra Pty Ltd., NZ** and **SnapFashun Inc**.*

4. kids bodysuits and jackets

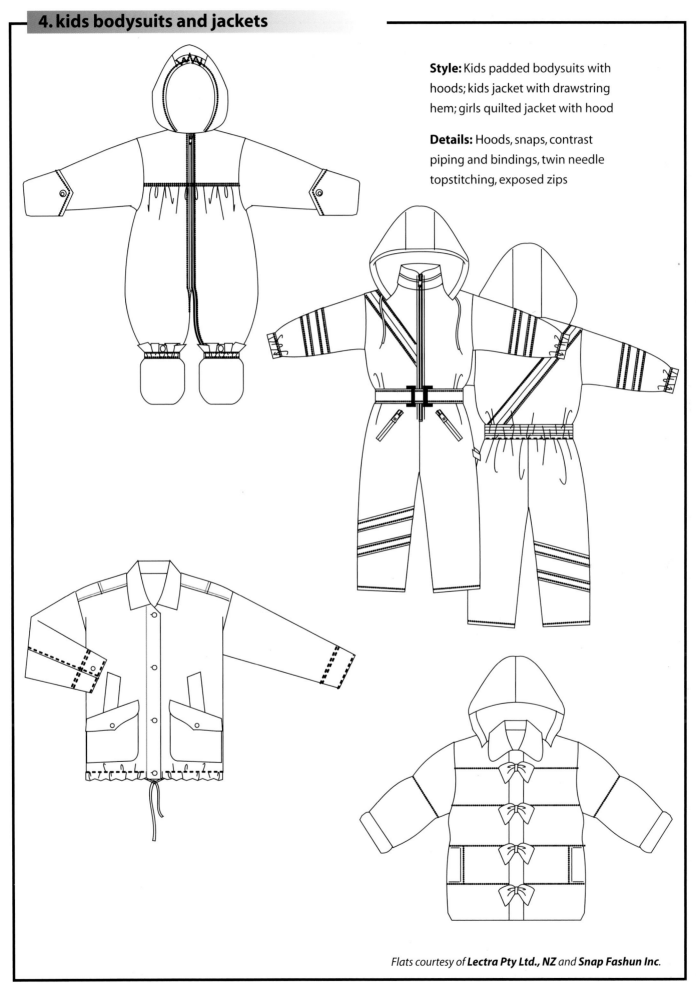

Style: Kids padded bodysuits with hoods; kids jacket with drawstring hem; girls quilted jacket with hood

Details: Hoods, snaps, contrast piping and bindings, twin needle topstitching, exposed zips

*Flats courtesy of **Lectra Pty Ltd., NZ** and **Snap Fashun Inc**.*

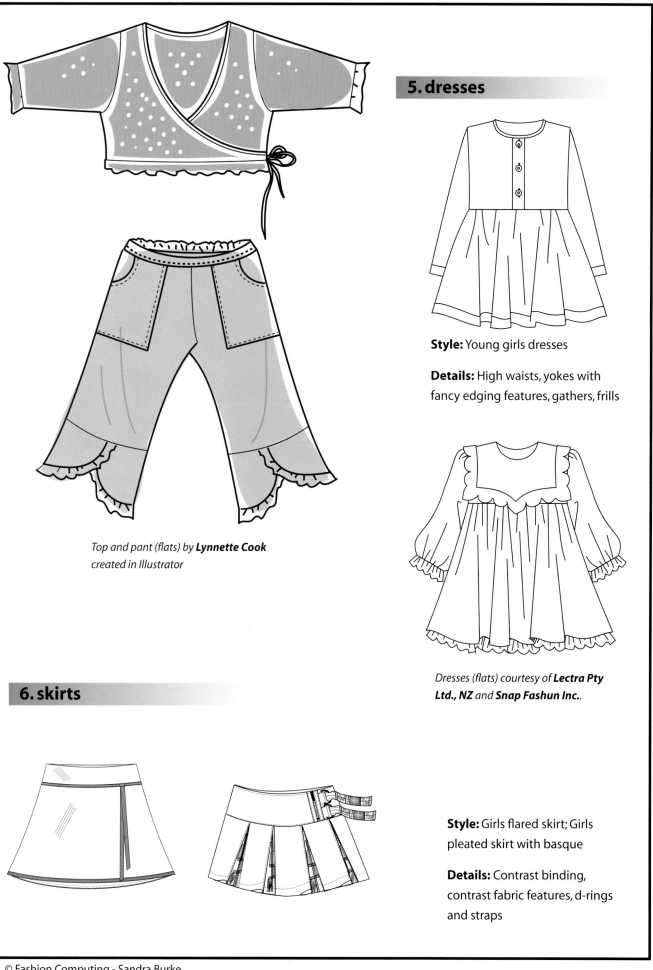

*Top and pant (flats) by **Lynnette Cook** created in Illustrator*

5. dresses

Style: Young girls dresses

Details: High waists, yokes with fancy edging features, gathers, frills

*Dresses (flats) courtesy of **Lectra Pty Ltd., NZ** and **Snap Fashun Inc.**.*

6. skirts

Style: Girls flared skirt; Girls pleated skirt with basque

Details: Contrast binding, contrast fabric features, d-rings and straps

7. tops, shirts and blouses

Style: Kids tops, shirts and blouses

Details: Contrast bindings, flat lock stitching on stretch fabrics, twin needle topstitching, bias trim features, frills, wraps

*Top (flat) by **Lynnette Cook**
created in Illustrator*

*Flats courtesy of **Lectra Pty Ltd., NZ** and **Snap Fashun Inc.***

scanning and digital photography

*Fashion presentation by **Frances Howie***
Ink on paper, scanned illustrations, digital photographs, edited in Photoshop

Scanners and digital cameras perform one main function - capture images and digitise them into a computer. These digitised images can then be edited and manipulated, to embellish design work before being printed out, used on the Web, or published. This chapter explains how fashion designers use scans and digitised images as part of the fashion design process.

Digitised images visually communicate design information, enhance creativity and add personal style to design work from mood boards to fabric, color, design, fashion illustrations and flats. You can capture and digitise images such as:

- Fashion shows/exhibitions/displays - record the latest trends, fabrics, colors
- Catwalk shows, street fashion, store reports
- Fabrics - a swatch of fabric can be used to 'fill' a flat or fashion illustration with pattern, or used to create a fabric presentation
- Small objects e.g. buttons, trims, jewellery
- Your personal fashion collections, clothing and artwork - use this as part of your digital design portfolio and CV.

Fashion designers frequently use digital cameras (and mobile phone cameras), especially when they are on fashion resource, buying or manufacturing trips, to visually communicate design information back to the design office. This keeps the wheels of the competitive fashion world turning even faster to get the latest fashion merchandise into store.

scanning tips

Before scanning an image you should have an idea of what the image is to be used for, and have a target size in mind. This way you will be able to select a suitable image mode, resolution and scale to achieve clean, sharp quality images.

Scanned flats and fashion illustrations that are to be filled with color and pattern should be drawn using clear, well defined lines, with all paths closed (line ends joined) (see *Photoshop Color and Effects*, exercise 6b, to close a path with the Pencil Tool).

'Accessories' illustrations hand drawn, scanned and edited in Photoshop and Illustrator - created by Alissa Stytsenko-Berdnik

step1

To create a scan from within Photoshop
- Choose File (Menu Bar)>Import and either; select Twain_32 or select the appropriate device from the sub-menu (to take you into your scanning software) (You can also follow the instructions that come with your scanner to open the scanning program and scan an image.)

step 2 - image mode/type

Select how the image is to be captured (see *Computer Basics* chapter):

- **RGB mode** - scan colour photographs, rendered fashion illustrations and flats, magazine tear-outs, fabrics etc.
- **Grayscale mode** - scan any of the above items, including black and white photographs
- **Lineart** - scan line drawings, single-color drawings (flats, fashion illustrations), logos, text (also photographs for effect).

When scanning several images at once, the output will be better if you select similar images e.g. dark images with other dark images, light images with light images.

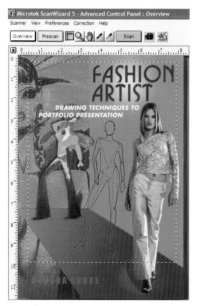

Settings Panel from the scanner software, displaying steps 2-5

Preview panel from the scanner software, displaying the frame and the section of the image that will be captured (the settings above apply to this image)

step 3 - resolution and scale

Select the required resolution and scale (see *Computer Basics* chapter):

- Resolution - 72 to 96 dpi (web), 150 - 200 dpi (inkjet, deskjet printers), 300 dpi (commercial work)
- Scale - 50%, 100%, 200% etc. - scan the biggest and best original (an image will lose its sharpness the more it is scaled up from the original)
- Scanning an image at too high a resolution, and larger than required, captures more pixels than necessary, and creates an unnecessarily large file size
- A scanned image may be scaled up or down using Photoshop (image editing software), but this can cause loss of quality and sharpness. Try to keep within a 10% margin or rescan the image to the required size.

step 4 descreen

An undesirable moiré (pattern) can appear when scanning glossy magazine images. As a guide to prevent this happening choose:

- descreen off - colour, and black and white photographs, objects
- descreen on - for glossy magazines/books, newspapers.

step 5 - preview

Preview the image to check the area to be scanned is captured within the scanning frame (the frame can be scaled up or down, and dragged to position).

step 6 - editing features

Use image editing software such as Photoshop (industry standard) to edit your digitised images to rotate, adjust colors, sharpen, etc. This way there is more control over the final result (see *Photoshop - Color and Effects* chapter).

- Use the best quality originals available. Image editing software can be used to clean up, sharpen, close paths with a pencil line, and retouch images, but it takes that extra time and effort to do so.

step 7 - large images

To capture large pieces of artwork that are too big for the scanner, you can:

- Take a digital photograph of the artwork and transfer the image into your computer (a tripod is best used here to keep the camera steady) (recommended)
- Scan the artwork in sections, join the images in an image editing program, then use the tools to remove unwanted joins to achieve a perfect piece of artwork (or you could experiment with Photomerge in Photoshop).

step 8 - scan

- Click the Scan button.
- Once the scan is finished, the image appears in Photoshop, save as a PSD (Photoshop), TIFF or JPEG etc. (see *Computer Basics* chapter).

digital photography tips

Digital cameras take photographs in JPEG format (see *Computer Basics* chapter). I suggest you use the highest resolution photographs your camera can capture in JPEG format as this gives you the best option as to their output (printing or Web). A captured image will never be better than the one that the camera has originally saved. 'Resampling up' an image (making an image larger in Photoshop) involves interpolation (adding pixels) and does not increase the quality and detail, but can actually lose detail and sharpness.

After an image is transferred to the computer, it can be opened in an image editing program, e.g. Photoshop, and should be immediately saved as a TIFF (or .psd for Photoshop). This way no more detail is lost with the JPEG image compression file format (see *Computer Basics* chapter).

Some cameras have the option to take a RAW or TIFF format image, but these formats take up massive amounts of memory and a large memory card is required to save RAW images. (JPEG format should be adequate for your fashion projects.)

Photographer - Louise Davies, model - Esther.
Take digital photographs of your collections, use them in presentations and save them in your digital portfolio.

digitised images

Save your images so that you can retrieve them easily e.g. in the *My Pictures* Folder, and create subfolders for the various image categories (see *Computer Basics* chapter). The images can be:

- Edited and manipulated in your image editing software e.g. Photoshop
- Imported into drawing packages e.g. Illustrator, CorelDRAW, Freehand
- Inserted as a picture in a PowerPoint presentation - screen slide show or video presentation
- Used in a website or sent as an email attachment
- Inserted as a picture in a word processing package e.g. Microsoft Word

This chapter has explained some key techniques for scanning and digital photography as part of the fashion design process. It helps form the foundation for creating your design presentations in the following chapters and exercises, where your digitised images will be edited and manipulated.

Fashion illustration (hand drawn) and fabric scanned and edited in Photoshop, created by Stuart McKenzie

*An **instructor's manual** with exercises will be available for lecturers, see <www.knowledgezone.net>*

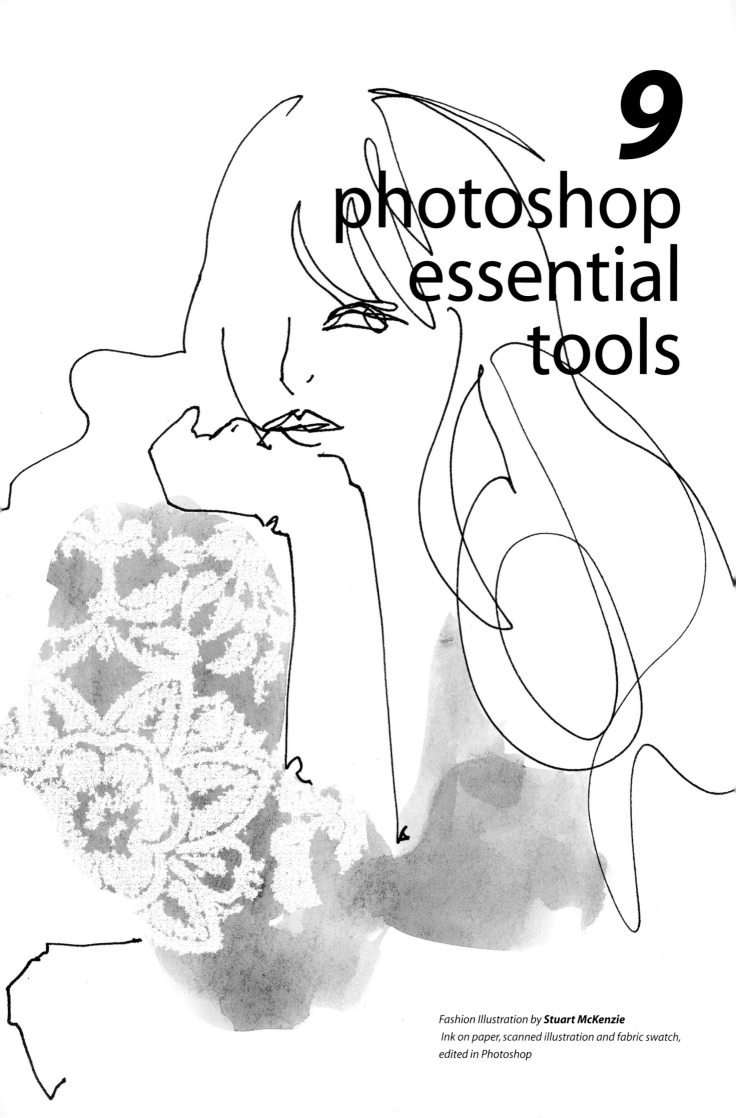

9
photoshop
essential
tools

Fashion Illustration by **Stuart McKenzie**
Ink on paper, scanned illustration and fabric swatch,
edited in Photoshop

Photoshop is the market standard image editing software. Fashion Designers use Photoshop to edit images to create presentation material and embellish design illustrations. These images include fashion illustrations, flats, fabrics and trims, photographs and magazine clippings.

This chapter explains how to use 10 essential image editing techniques, tools and commands. Figure 9.1 presents an overview of these techniques and outlines the structure of this chapter. This is an excellent reference guide to refer to as you work though the following exercises and chapters.

techniques	exercises/tools/commands
1. Create a New File	1. Create a New Blank Image
2. Open an Image	2. Open an Image Using the File Browser
3. View and Move Around an Image	3a. View Command 3b. Zoom Tool 3c. Hand Tool 3d. Navigator Palette 3e. Scroll Bars
4. Rotate an Image	4. Rotate a Scanned Image
5. Crop an Image	5. Crop a Photograph
6. Change Canvas Size	6. Increase the Canvas Size of an Image
7. Return an Image to a Previous State	7a. History Palette 7b. Edit Command 7c. Revert Command
8. Make Selections	8a. Marquee Tools - Rectangular Marquee Tool, Elliptical Marquee Tool 8b. Lasso Tools - Regular Lasso Tool, Polygonal Lasso Tool, Magnetic Lasso Tool 8c. Magic Wand 8d. Options for Marquee Tools 8e. Color Range Command
9. Manipulate Selections	9a. Move a Selection Using the Move Tool 9b. Copy and Paste a Selection Using the Move Tool and Commands
10. Working with Layers	10a. Scale Down a Fashion Illustration on a Layer 10b. Change the Opacity of a Photograph on a Layer

Figure 9.1
Table of Photoshop exercises

work area

The starting point for Photoshop is the work area, Figure 9.2. - all image editing software will have a similar arrangement. The image editing tools and commands for this chapter are selected from the **Tool Box, Menu Bar, Options Bar** and the **Palettes** which appear within the Work Area.

options bar: displays options to customize tools from the toolbox e.g. if a Selection Tool (Toolbox) is selected the Options Bar displays choices for adding or deleting from a selection etc. (here the Rectangular Marquee Tool was selected).

menu bar: displays menu commands - click on a menu heading to display a drop down menu.

palettes: are small moveable windows that display common commands and resources e.g. Navigator, Color, History, Layers - choose 'window' (Menu Bar) to display a drop down menu and select a palette (a 'check/tick mark' next to the palette name confirms it is selected). Click on the tabs for palette options.

toolbox: displays the tools for creating and editing images as tool icons - click on the tool's icon to select the tool. A small triangle next to the icon indicates related hidden tools - click on it to open and select more tools.

active image area (window): is the area where the image is created and edited

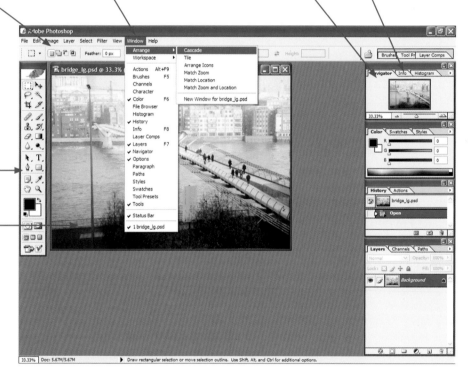

Figure 9.2
Photoshop Work Area displaying a typical image editing layout with Options Bar, Menu Bar, Palettes, Toolbox and Active Image Area

Tool tips - position the pointer over a tool to display the tool's icon, name and short-cut (short-cuts are great for tools most frequently used e.g. click 'Z' for the Zoom tool).

Photoshop toolbox

This Photoshop toolbox identifies the tools and hidden tools used in this chapter and is a useful reference as you work through the exercises.

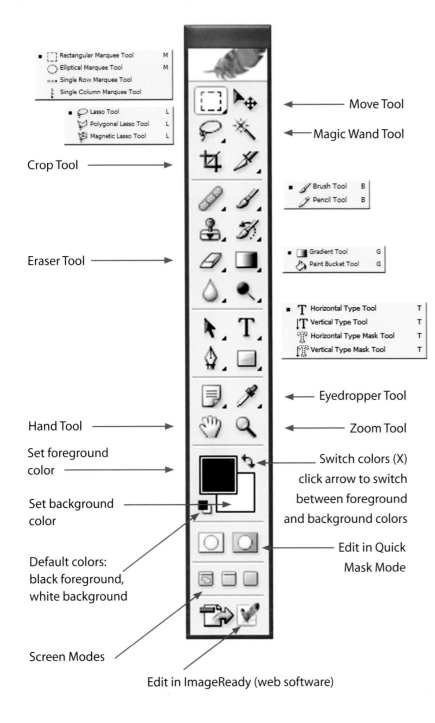

Rectangular Marquee Tool · M
Elliptical Marquee Tool · M
Single Row Marquee Tool
Single Column Marquee Tool

Lasso Tool · L
Polygonal Lasso Tool · L
Magnetic Lasso Tool · L

Move Tool

Magic Wand Tool

Crop Tool

Brush Tool · B
Pencil Tool · B

Gradient Tool · G
Paint Bucket Tool · G

Eraser Tool

Horizontal Type Tool · T
Vertical Type Tool · T
Horizontal Type Mask Tool · T
Vertical Type Mask Tool · T

Eyedropper Tool

Hand Tool

Zoom Tool

Set foreground color

Switch colors (X) click arrow to switch between foreground and background colors

Set background color

Default colors: black foreground, white background

Edit in Quick Mask Mode

Screen Modes

Edit in ImageReady (web software)

Help! - if you hit a problem and need more information use the 'Help' (Menu Bar) - it is a great reference guide and the more you use it the easier technical issues become.

Help
Photoshop Help...   F1
Welcome Screen...
About Photoshop...

About Plug-In   ▶

Export Transparent Image...
Resize Image...

System Info...

Activate...
Updates...
Registration...
Photoshop Online...

How to Create Web Images   ▶
How to Customize and Automate   ▶
How to Fix and Enhance Photos   ▶
How to Paint and Draw   ▶
How to Prepare Art for Other Applications ▶
How to Print Photos   ▶
How to Work with Color   ▶
How to Work with Layers and Selections ▶
How to Work with Type   ▶

How to Create How Tos   ▶

10 key fashion image editing techniques

The following 10 essential fashion image editing techniques are set out here as step-by-step exercises and are the starting point to manipulate and edit fashion illustrations, flats and presentations. These techniques will be developed further in *Photoshop Color and Effects,* and *Design Presentations.*

1. create a new file

You can create a new file with a blank canvas to start a design project.

Exercise 1: *Create a new blank image.*

1. Click File (Menu Bar)>New (the New dialog box appears)

2. Type a name for the new file, click on the down arrow to choose a 'Preset' (page size) or enter values for the Dimensions, select a Resolution, select a Color Mode (for more information see *Computer Basics* chapter) and Background Contents color. It is very important to set the correct resolution that you will be working with to avoid problems later.

3. A new image window is created and the name appears in its title bar.

2. open an image

To open an existing file you can use the File Browser, which is excellent for also managing your files; or choose File (Menu Bar)>Open (and locate the file from the menu).

Exercise 2: *Open an image using the File Browser.*

1. Choose File (Menu Bar)>Browse (the File Browser opens)

2. Click on the arrows to locate the folder containing your images e.g. *My Pictures* (the folder containing the scanned files from the *Scanning and Digital Photography* chapter).

3. Double click on a thumbnail image to open it.

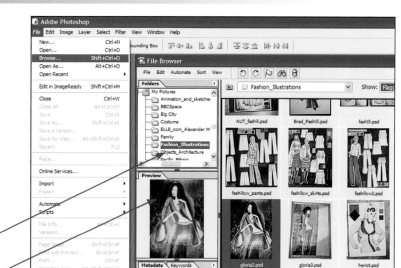

NOTE *When you open the image it appears on a background layer (see Layers in the* Computer Basics, *Chapter 3).*

3. view and move around an image

To edit an image you will need to 'view' and 'move' around the image window using various commands and tools e.g. the 'View' command, Zoom Tool, Hand Tool, Navigator Palette, Scroll Bars, and Rulers and Guides (see *Basic Drawing Techniques* chapter, exercise 2 and 15).

Exercise: 3a, 3b: *View an image using the View command and Zoom Tool.*

3a. View commands
• Choose View (Menu Bar), and select a command from the menu: Zoom In, Zoom Out (options are Fit on Screen, Actual Pixels, Screen Mode, Rulers, Snap To).

3b. Zoom Tool
• Select the Zoom Tool (Toolbox) and click the area you wish to zoom in on (excellent for zooming really close for editing fine details)
• To Zoom out - with the zoom tool selected, press 'Alt'.

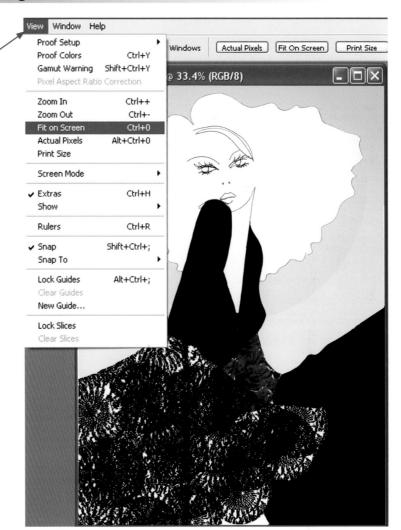

Exercise 3c, 3d and 3e: *Move around an image using the Hand Tool, Navigator palette and Scroll bars.*

In the 'Zoom In' mode, use the Hand Tool and Navigator palette to move around the image, use the scroll bars to view areas of the image using the same magnification.

3c. Hand Tool (zoom in first)
• Select the Hand Tool (Toolbox)
• Position the cursor over the image, click and drag to view another area of the image.

3d. Navigator Palette (zoom in first)
• Choose Window (Menu Bar)>Navigator (to display the palette)
• Drag the red frame in the palette to view another area of the image.

3e. Scroll bars (zoom in first)
• Click on the vertical or horizontal bars to move the view of the image up or down.

4. rotate an image

The Rotate Canvas command is used to rotate an image, e.g. a scanned image or an image from a digital camera to the correct orientation.

90 degrees CCW

Exercise 4: *Rotate a scanned image.*

1. Open an image
2. Select Image (Menu Bar)>Rotate Canvas
3. Choose one of the options from the drop down menu.

'CW' - clockwise, 'CCW' - counter clockwise, Arbitrary means you can adjust by whatever value you wish and is especially useful if an image is just slightly skew, even as little as 0.1!

```
180°
90° CW
90° CCW
Arbitrary...

Flip Canvas Horizontal
Flip Canvas Vertical
```

5. crop an image

The Crop Tool is used to remove an unwanted area of an image - this also helps to reduce the file size which in turn increases processing speed.

Exercise 5: *Crop a photograph.*

 1. Open an image (this could also be a fashion illustration etc.)
2. Select the Crop Tool (Toolbox)
3. Click and drag over the image to select the area you wish to keep
4. Click and drag the side and corner handles to adjust to the desired size of the crop area (click inside the cropping boundary box to move it without adjusting the size).

5. To complete the crop, click either 'Commit' or 'Cancel' commands (Options Bar), or press Enter (Return)

 'Snap' and 'Snap To' helps precise placement of cropping, selections and paths etc. To disable snapping choose View (Menu Bar) and deselect the check next to the command.

6. change the canvas size

The canvas (the area on which an image is placed) can be adjusted to add canvas above, below, to the right/ left, or around the whole image e.g. to create a larger canvas on which to place fabric swatches, a color story, or flats next to an illustration.

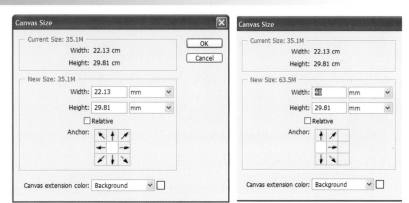

Exercise 6: *Increase the canvas size to the right side of an image.*

1. Open an image
2. Choose Image (Menu Bar)>Canvas Size (the Canvas Size dialog box appears, listing the dimensions and color of the canvas, the white box indicates the image's position)
3. Click on the arrow to the left of the white box to move it left; enter the new canvas size (40 cms was added to the width for this exercise, the height was not added to)
4. The canvas to the right of the image is increased.

7. return an image to a previous state

The History palette, Undo and Revert commands undo actions by returning the image to a previous state.

Exercise 7a, 7b, 7c: *Use the History palette, or the Edit, or Revert commands to return to a previous state.*

7a. History palette: Choose Window (Menu Bar)>History (to display the History palette)
• Click and drag the slider upward to select the state you wish to revert to (note states below are dimmed and will be discarded if you continue to work as selected).
7b. Edit command: Choose Edit (Menu Bar)>Step Forward to redo a stage of work. Choose Edit (Menu Bar)>Step Backward to undo a stage of work.
7c. Revert command: Choose File (Menu Bar)>Revert

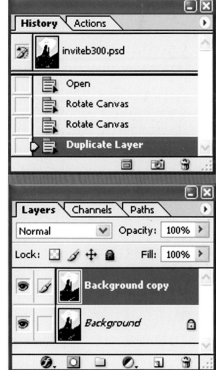

The History palette keeps a record of the last 20 modifications of an image, the most recent at the bottom of the palette.

8. make selections

When you select an area, a dotted, flashing outline, known as 'marching ants', surrounds the selection indicating that it is 'active' and any editing will only affect that area.

One of the most important techniques in Photoshop is making selections because this is the 'starting point' for editing and manipulating your images.

There are a number of selection tools and commands which can be used to select part or all of an image e.g. the sleeves of a garment, the complete garment, or the whole illustration. When you make a selection within an image, the remainder of the image will be left untouched. The three main selection tools are;

- Marquee Tools
- Lasso Tools
- Magic Wand Tool

8a. marquee tools

The Marquee Tools are subdivide into the:

- Rectangular Marquee Tool
- Elliptical Tool

8ai. The **Rectangular Marquee Tool** is used to make rectangular selections e.g. useful for creating fabric swatches, and color swatches arranged on a presentation.

Exercise 8ai: *Create a rectangular selection on a fabric swatch.*

1. Open an image of a scanned fabric

2. Select the Rectangular Marquee Tool (Toolbox)

3. Click and drag to define the area you wish to select (to select a square, hold 'Shift' as you drag)

4. With the selection still active, click and drag in the selection to move it around the image.

5. Deselect by clicking inside or outside the selection marquee, or, Choose Select (Menu Bar)>Deselect.

Use the Options Bar to change the way the marquee tools select e.g. set the exact size for a selection - choose Fixed size, and enter values for width and height - use this when selecting fabric or color swatches that need to be the same size for a Design Presentation.

| Style: | Fixed Size | Width: | 300 px | ⇄ | Height: | 300 px |

8aii. The **Elliptical Marquee Tool** is used to make elliptical selections e.g. useful for highlighting a design detail on a presentation.

Exercise 8aii: *Make an elliptical selection on a 'flat'.*

1. Open an image of a flat

 2. Select the Elliptical Marquee Tool (Toolbox)

3. Click and drag to define the area you wish to select (to select a circle, hold down 'Shift' as you drag)

These selections will be developed in the Design Presentation chapter.

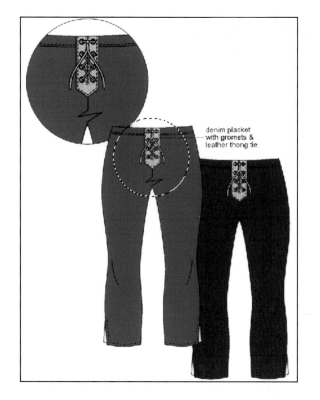

denim placket with gromets & leather thong tie

8b. lasso tools

The *Lasso Tools* are subdivided into the:
- Regular Lasso Tool
- Polygonal Tool
- Magnetic Lasso Tool

Lasso Tools are used to make irregular shaped selections e.g. select a fashion illustration, part of a photograph, an object.

8bi. The **regular Lasso Tool** is used to make curved selections.

Exercise 8bi: *Select a fashion illustration using the regular Lasso Tool .*

1. Open an image of a fashion illustration

2. Select the regular Lasso Tool (Toolbox)

3. Click and drag around the fashion illustration to make the selection
4. Release the cursor at the start point to complete the selection.

Regular_Lasso_Woman.psd ...

8bii. The **Polygonal Lasso Tool** is used to make straight-edge selections.

Exercise 8bii: *Select a fashion figure/ illustration using the Polygonal Lasso Tool.*

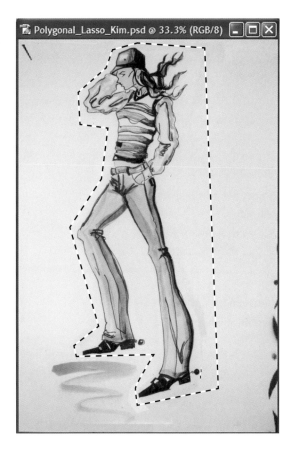

Polygonal_Lasso_Kim.psd @ 33.3% (RGB/8)

1. Click and hold the triangle on the regular Lasso Tool (Toolbox), select the Polygonal Lasso Tool in the box as it appears

2. Position the cursor over the image

3. Click, move the cursor, click; repeat until the area is selected

4. Finish at the start point with a click (the cursor icon changes to indicate that the start point is reached)

5. If you double click to end the selection before reaching the start point a straight line will immediately connect the two points.

8biii. The **Magnetic Lasso Tool** is used to make 'snap-to' selections, particularly useful when the image to be selected contrasts strongly with the background.

Exercise 8biii: *To select a section of a photograph to be used as a background for a presentation.*

Magnetic_Lasso_Flowers.psd @ 33.3...

1. Click and hold the triangle on the regular Lasso Tool (Toolbox), select the Magnetic Lasso Tool in the box as it appears

2. Click on the edge of the image to place the first 'fastening point'

3. Drag the cursor along the area you want to select - this creates more 'fastening points' which 'snap to' the 'strongest' edge of the image

4. Finish at the start point with a click to complete the selection.

Use the Zoom Tool to zoom into a selection when you have an intricate image selection to create (see exercise 3).

8c. magic wand tool

The **Magic Wand Tool** is used to select similar colored areas in an image, e.g. remove a fashion illustration from its background and drag it on to another image/design presentation.

Exercise 8c: *Select the background of a fashion illustration using the Magic Wand Tool and inverse it.*

1. Select the Magic Wand Tool (Toolbox)

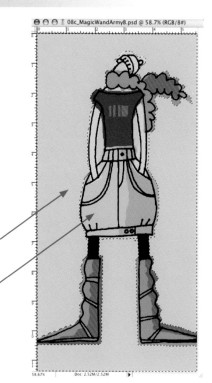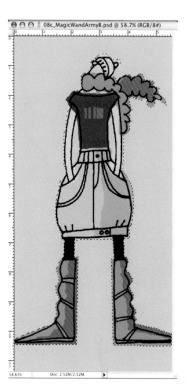

2. Click on the background to make the selection

3. Choose Select (Menu Bar)>Inverse (the fashion illustration is now selected). (This technique will be used as part of exercise 9bii.)

4. To delete the selection, press the 'Delete' key.

The **Options Bar** provides options as to the way the Marquee tools work.

8d. options for marquee tools

Exercise 8d: *Add to a selection*

1. Select any of the Marquee tools (Toolbox) (in this case the Magic Wand Tool was selected

2. Click on the background to make the selection

3. Click the 'Add to selection' button (Options Bar)

4. Continue to select more of the image (every time you click, you add to the selection)

5. To delete from a selection, click 'Subtract from selection' (Options Bar).

• **Also:** *Add to a selection by holding down Shift while drawing an additional selection - Delete from a selection by holding down Alt while drawing a selection*

• **Also:** *Choose Select (Menu Bar)>Grow (to grow the selection within the boundaries) or Similar (to select all the pixels within the color range)*

Options Bar for Selection Tools (the tool that is being used is displayed - in this case, the Magic Wand Tool)

• **Tolerance** *low numbers select a limited range of color (pixels); high numbers select a wider range of color (pixels).*

Options Bar for Selection Tools (the tool that is being used is displayed - in this case, the Magnetic Tool)

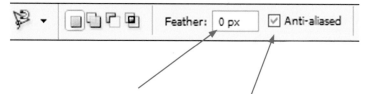

• **Feather** *to soften the edges of the selection*

• **Anti-aliased** *to smooth the jagged edges of a bitmap selection (bitmaps are made up of thousands of square pixels, see Computer Basics chapter).*

© Fashion Computing - Sandra Burke

8e. color range command

The **Color Range** command is used to quickly select a region of relatively solid color e.g. select the background of a complex line drawing to which you wish to add a background color.

Exercise 8e: *Select the background of a line drawing using the Color Range command.*

1. Choose Select (Menu Bar)>Color Range (the Color Range dialog box appears)
2. Click inside the image window (in this case the bird image) to select pixels/color (here the white background was 'clicked')
3. Photoshop selects all the pixels in the image that are similar to the pixel clicked
4. Click OK ('marching ants' indicate the selection has been created and can then be edited).

To select all the pixels (the entire image), choose Select (Menu Bar)>All

The Quick Mask Mode icon (Toolbox) creates a semi-transparent overlay which protects the area - see the Help (Menu Bar) for more information.

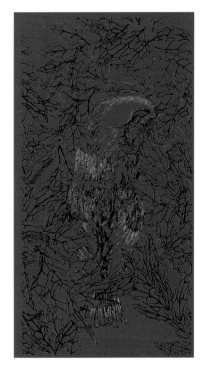

Once the selection is made, the color of the selection can then be changed (see Chapter 10, Photoshop Color and Effects exercise 1-3)

9. manipulate selections

Once a selection has been made it can be manipulated e.g. moved, deleted, copied and pasted, extracted, skewed, distorted, rotated or scaled, etc.

9a. move a selection

The Move Tool is used to move a selection allowing you to rearrange elements on the background layer or on to a new layer. The Move Tool is also used to move selections, layers and reposition guides.

Exercise 9a: *Select and move a fashion illustration on its background layer.*

1. Open an image
2. Create a selection (here the Polygonal Lasso Tool was used, see exercise 8bii)

 3. Select the Move Tool (Toolbox)
4. Click inside the selection and drag it to move it within the image window
5. The original location of the selection fills with the current background color.

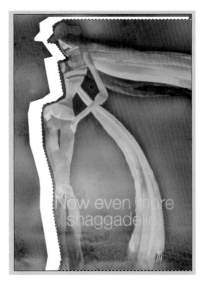

 Always SELECT the image, part of the image or layer that you wish to edit and manipulate, e.g. move, copy, resize, re color, scale up

9b. copy and paste a selection

The 'Copy and Paste' technique creates a duplicate of a selection within the same image, or from one image to another e.g. useful when presenting copies of a flat to display color or fabric choices, or to copy a fashion illustration on to a background image.

Exercise 9bi: *Copy and paste a scanned flat within the same image area.*

1. Open an image of a flat (if necessary, increase the canvas size to accommodate an identical flat, see exercise 6)

2. Create a selection using one of the Selection Tools (Toolbox), (the regular Lasso Tool was used here as per exercise 8bi)

3. Select the Move Tool (Toolbox) and hold down 'Alt' (option) while you click within the selection and drag it to another part of the image

4. Release the cursor to 'drop' the selection on the image

A duplicate of the selection is created in the new location on the same layer

Or, after making a selection, use commands - choose Edit (Menu Bar)>Copy, Edit (Menu Bar)>Paste (this creates a new layer), and then use the Move tool to move the copy.

If you use the lasso tool you will pick up everything (pixels) within the selection e.g in this selection the white area around the flat. Use the Magic Wand Tool or Magnetic Lasso Tool to select the flat only.

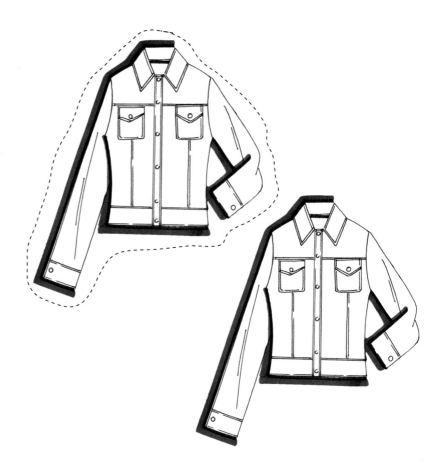

Exercise 9bii: *Copy and paste a scanned fashion illustration on to another image.*

1. Open the source image (the fashion illustration to be copied and pasted), and open the destination image (here the destination image is the scan of London's walking bridge with canvas increased)

2. Create a selection of the fashion illustration (the Magnetic Lasso exercise 8biii was used to here to select the background, then Select (Menu Bar)>Inverse to select the fashion illustration)

3. Select the Move Tool (Toolbox)

4. Click and drag the selection into the destination image window (the walking bridge)

5. A duplicate of the selection is created in the new location on its own layer - choose Window (Menu Bar)> Layer (to display the Layers palette)

6. Or, after making a selection, use the commands, choose Edit (Menu Bar)>Copy, Edit (Menu Bar)>Paste - this also creates a new layer in the destination.

Source image (this is the image to be selected and moved to the destination image)

Destination image (this is the image for the background for the presentation). The canvas has been increased above the photo (see exercise 6)

When dragging one image to another image the resolution should be the same - if not you will find the technique will not work as expected.

When you copy an image to another image a new layer is created

Layers can be renamed - this is especially useful when you work on complex presentations with many layers.

Choose Window (Menu Bar)>Layers (to display the Layers palette), click on the layer you want to rename and in the Layers palette, click on the arrow, upper right (to display the Layer options), click on Layer Properties (to display the pop-up dialog box) and type in the new name, click OK.

10. working with layers

Working with layers gives you a great deal of flexibility e.g. a layer may be scaled, rotated, skewed, distorted, its transparency changed without affecting the other layers in the image.

Exercise 10a: *Scale down a fashion illustration on a layer.*

Continue with the previous exercise 9bii, choose Window (Menu Bar)>Layers (to display the Layers palette)
1. Click in the layers palette and select the 'fashion illustration' layer
2. Choose Edit (Menu Bar)>Transform>Scale (a rectangular bounding box, with handles, surrounds the selection)
3. To scale in proportion hold 'Shift' as you click and drag a corner handle

 4. Click the Commit button (Options Bar), or press Enter
5. The fashion illustration will now be smaller but the background remains the same size.

 If for some reason your images are unexpectedly very different in size when you move them, check that the resolutions are the same e.g the photo at 300 dpi and the fashion illustration at 72 dpi would give you a small fashion illustration against the bridge

 To rotate a selection, select the image layer, choose Select (Menu Bar)>Rotate, click and drag the bounding box bi-directional arrows in a circular direction.

Exercise 10b: *Change the opacity of a photograph on a layer.*

Continue with the previous exercise 10a, choose Window (Menu Bar)>Layers (to display the Layers palette)
1. Click in the Layers palette and select the 'photograph' layer (the bridge) and in the Layers palette reduce the Opacity (here 50% was used).

This chapter has explained how to use 10 essential image editing techniques, tools and commands. These skills form the foundation for the following chapter, *Photoshop Color and Effects* and for creating fashion presentations in Chapter 11, *Design Presentations.*

*An **instructor's manual** with exercises will be available for lecturers, see www.knowledgezone.net*

10

photoshop color and effects

Fashion Illustration by **Stuart McKenzie**
Ink on paper, scanned illustration and images, edited in Photoshop

The previous chapter *Photoshop Essential Tools* gave you the starting point to manipulate and edit fashion illustrations, flats and presentations. This chapter explains how to further develop your images using 11 key image editing techniques for working with color and pattern, and to create effects. Figure. 10.1 presents an overview of these techniques and outlines the structure of this chapter. This is an excellent reference guide to refer to as you work though the following exercises and chapters. These techniques will be developed further in the *Design Presentations* chapter.

techniques	exercises
1. Select Foreground and Background Colors	1a. Set the Foreground Color Using the Color Picker Palette 1b. Set the Background Color Using the Color Picker Palette 1c. Select a Color Using the Eyedropper Tool
2. The Swatches Palette	2a. Set Colors Using the Swatches Palette 2b. Add a Color to the Swatches Palette 2c. Delete a Color from the Swatches Palette 2d. Reset the Swatches Palette
3. Fill a Selection with Color	3a. Fill a Flat with Color 3b. Fill a Fashion Illustration with Color
4. Fill a Selection with a Gradient	4a. Fill the Background of a Flat with a Gradient
5. Fill a Selection with a Pattern	5a. Define a Pattern 5b. Fill a Flat with a Pattern
6. Paint and Draw with Color	6a. Paint with the Brush Tool 6b. Close a Path with the Pencil Tool
7. Stroke a Selection	7a. Stroke a Fashion Illustration 7b. Stroke a Fabric Swatch
8. Erase Elements/Pixels	8a. Erase Marks from a Scanned Fashion Illustration
9. Filters	9a. Sharpen a Scanned Photograph 9b. Sharpen a Scanned Fashion Illustration 9c. Create a Draped Look to a Garment 9d. Experiment with Filters and Image Color Effects
10. Create and Edit Type	10a. Create Type 10b. Create Type in a Bounding Box 10c. Create a Drop Shadow, an Inner Glow, and Warp Type 10d. Change the Opacity of Type 10e. Rasterize and Apply a Filter to Type 10f. Fill Type with a Pattern 10g. Fill Type with a Gradient
11. Create Layer Styles	11. Create a Color Overlay on a Flat

Figure 10.1
Table of Photoshop Color and Effects exercises

1. select foreground and background colors

In Photoshop you can select and work with two colors at a time - the foreground color and the background color.

- The foreground color is applied when you use the Paint Bucket, Line, Pencil, Brush and Type Tools.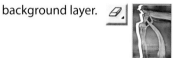
- The background color is applied when you use the Eraser Tool, and when a selection is moved or deleted from a background layer.

- To revert to the default background and foreground colors, click the Default Colors Icon

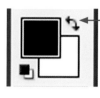

- To switch between the foreground and background colors, click on the Switch Foreground and Background Colors arrow.

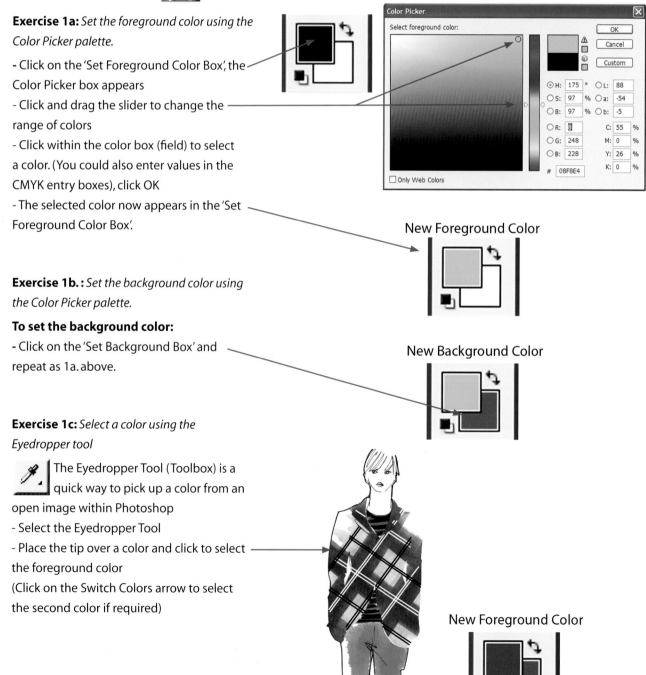

Exercise 1a: *Set the foreground color using the Color Picker palette.*

- Click on the 'Set Foreground Color Box', the Color Picker box appears
- Click and drag the slider to change the range of colors
- Click within the color box (field) to select a color. (You could also enter values in the CMYK entry boxes), click OK
- The selected color now appears in the 'Set Foreground Color Box'.

New Foreground Color

Exercise 1b. : *Set the background color using the Color Picker palette.*

To set the background color:
- Click on the 'Set Background Box' and repeat as 1a. above.

New Background Color

Exercise 1c: *Select a color using the Eyedropper tool*

The Eyedropper Tool (Toolbox) is a quick way to pick up a color from an open image within Photoshop
- Select the Eyedropper Tool
- Place the tip over a color and click to select the foreground color
(Click on the Switch Colors arrow to select the second color if required)

New Foreground Color

2. the swatches palette

Exercise 2a: *Set colors using the Swatches palette.*

- Choose Window (Menu Bar)>Swatches (to display the Swatches palette)
- Click on a color to select the foreground color (the foreground color is now set)
- To select a background color, hold down press Ctrl (Command/Mac), and then click on a color swatch.

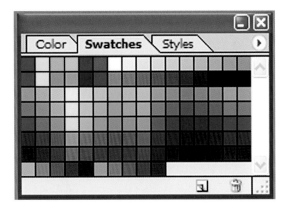

The Swatches palette will give you flat color. If there is any movement of shape/pattern a different technique is used, that is color hue and saturation

Exercise 2b: *Add a color to the Swatches palette.*

The Swatches palette can be customized by adding or deleting colors e.g. create a color palette for a new season's range.

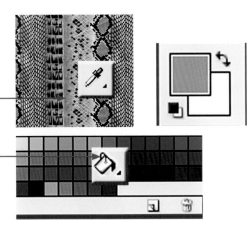

- Select the Eyedropper Tool
- Click on an image/color to select a new color
- Position the cursor over an empty area in the Swatches palette (the cursor changes to the Paint Bucket Tool)
- Click to add the color (the Color Swatch Name dialog box appears)
-Type a name for the new color swatch (in this case 'Snake brown')
- Click OK - the new color is now added to the Swatches palette.

Color Swatch Name

Name: Snake_brown   OK   Cancel

Exercise 2c: *Delete a color swatch from the Swatches palette.*

- Press Alt (Windows) or alt/option (Mac) and click on a color swatch (the scissors appear).

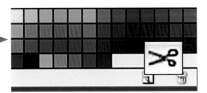

Exercise 2d: *Reset the Swatches palette.*

- Click the triangle to the right of the swatches tab (to display the Swatches palette menu)
- Select the 'Reset Swatches' to reset the palette to its default settings, or you can select another palette from the Swatches palette list (here 'Small Thumbnail' is checked to display the colors as small squares of color.)

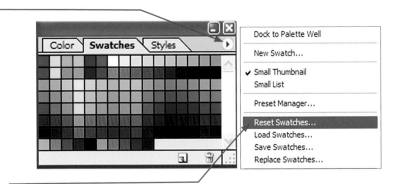

Dock to Palette Well

New Swatch...

✓ Small Thumbnail
Small List

Preset Manager...

Reset Swatches...
Load Swatches...
Save Swatches...
Replace Swatches...

3. fill a selection with color

To 'fill' a selection with color you can use the 'Fill' command or the Paint Bucket tool.
• The Fill command is used to fill an entire selected area.

• The Paint Bucket Tool is used to color pixels with the foreground color.

Exercise 3a: *Fill a flat with color.*

- Select the foreground and/or background colors

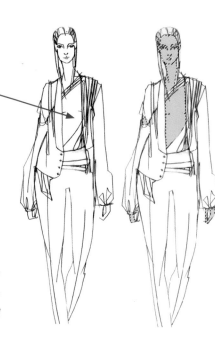

- Using one of the selection tools select the area(s) to be filled (the Magic Wand was used here to fill each section of the jacket)
- Choose Edit (Menu Bar)>Fill (the 'Fill' dialogue box appears)
- Select Foreground> Normal>100% (Opacity) (Note: there are numerous options with which to experiment.)
- Click OK
- The selection will be filled with the foreground color
- Deselect to finish.

Exercise 3b: *Fill a fashion illustration with color.*

- Follow the above steps making individual selections for the flesh, hair, clothing, etc.

To 'fill' a selection with color, or pattern, 'paths' must be 'closed paths' if not color will spill out like paint through a hole (see exercise 6b. to Close a Path with the Pencil Tool).

4. fill a selection with a gradient

The Gradient Tool is used to create a transition from one color to another. You can create multicolor gradients, Linear, Radial, Angle, Reflected and Diamond effects. Gradients can give a shaded or 3D look to an image or background.

Exercise 4a: *Fill the background of a flat with a gradient.*

- Define foreground and background colors
- Select the background of the flat image (the Magic Wand was used here)
- Select the Gradient Tool
- Choose a gradient type from the Options Bar (Linear was used here)
- Or click on the gradient swatch to display the Gradient Editor to choose a preset gradient (these can be customized)
- Position the cursor where you want the gradient to start, click and drag (the angle and distance you drag defines the direction and transition - dragging a short line produces an abrupt transition and vice versa)
- Deselect to finish.

© Fashion Computing - Sandra Burke

5. fill a selection with a pattern

To 'fill' a selection with a pattern, the pattern must first be defined. The pattern could be a scanned or computer generated fabric, or a pattern from the Fill preset.

Exercise 5a: *Define a pattern.*

- Open the file of the fabric to be used as the 'Fill'

- Select the Rectangular Marquee Tool

- Make the selection of the area of fabric to be defined

- Choose Edit (Menu Bar)>Define Pattern (the Pattern Name box appears), enter a name for the pattern

- Deselect to finish.

Exercise 5b: *Fill a flat with a pattern.*

- Select the area(s) to be filled (the Magic Wand was used here)

- Choose Edit (Menu Bar)>Fill (the Fill box appears)

- Click the 'Contents/Use' arrow, choose Pattern (the Custom Pattern box appears), click on the triangle to display the patterns and scroll to select the new pattern you have just defined)

- Click OK

- The selection will be filled with the pattern

- Deselect to finish.

 • *When 'filling' with a detailed or dark pattern, the style lines need to be drawn with a bold line to retain the detail.*

• *When a pattern is defined it will repeat itself throughout the selection to be filled, therefore, size and area selected is important e.g. if the Pattern fill is too large, you will need to scale the pattern before defining.*

• *Check out the Pattern Stamp Tool and the Pattern Maker (Filter) to create pattern - see Help (Menu Bar) for more information.*

6. paint and draw with color

The Brush Tool is used to paint strokes with softened edges; the Airbrush Tool (an option when using the Brush) paints soft lines that get darker as the mouse is held down, and the Pencil Tool paints hard-edged strokes.

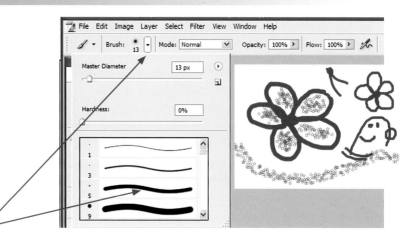

Exercise 6a: *Paint with the Brush Tool.*

 - Select the Brush Tool (Toolbox)
- Select foreground color (exercise 1)
- On the Options bar, click the triangle next to 'Brush' (to display the Brush palette)
- Select brush size, shape and type
- Click and drag to paint with the foreground color.

Brush styles can be to customized as a 'preset' brush allowing you to create your own collection of custom brushes.

The Pencil Tool can be used to close the path of a scanned flat or fashion illustration.

Exercise 6b: *Close a path with the Pencil Tool.*

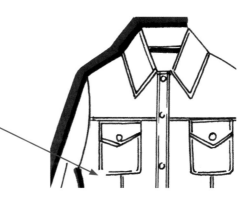

- Select the Zoom Tool (Toolbox) to zoom into the open path (*Photoshop Essential Tools,* exercise 3)

- Select foreground color (exercise 1)
- Select the Pencil Tool (Toolbox)
- Select from the Brush palette, size, type, opacity etc.
- Click and drag to draw a line and connect the open paths - navigate around the image to select all the open paths - when all paths are closed you will be able to fill the selections
- Deselect to finish
• To draw a **straight line**, press and hold Shift as you drag.
• Use the Pen Tool to create shapes and paths (*see Help (Menu Bar) for more information*).

7. stroke a selection

The 'Stroke' command is used to draw a line along the edge of a selection. This can be useful if you wish to enhance an image e.g. a fashion illustration that needs to stand out from the background.

Exercise 7a: *Stroke a fashion illustration.*

- Select the image using a selection tool (the Magic Wand tool was used here to select the background, then Select (Menu Bar)>Inverse (to select the fashion illustration, see *Photoshop Essential Tools*, exercise 8c)
- Choose Edit (Menu Bar)>Stroke (the Stroke box displays)
- Select from the Stroke box: enter a Width; select Inside, click the Color Box to define the stroke color, click Inside, Center or Outside stroke (4px, black, Outside, Normal, and 90% Opacity were selected here)
- Deselect to finish.

Exercise 7b: *Stroke a fabric swatch.*

- Repeat as above (20px, black, Inside, Normal, and 100% Opacity were selected here).

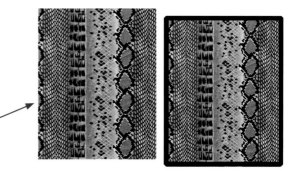

8. erase elements/pixels

The Eraser Tool is used to remove pixels (lines, marks, parts of an image). It erases using the background color when working on the Background layer.

Exercise 8a: *Erase marks from a scanned fashion illustration.*

- Select the background layer in the layers palette (in a newly scanned image the background layer is the only layer)

- Select the Eraser Tool
- On the Options bar, click the triangle next to 'Brush' (to display the Brush palette)
- Select brush size, shape and type
- Click Mode (Options Bar) to select the type of eraser (Block was used here)
- Click and drag inside the image (Photoshop erases the image using the background color).

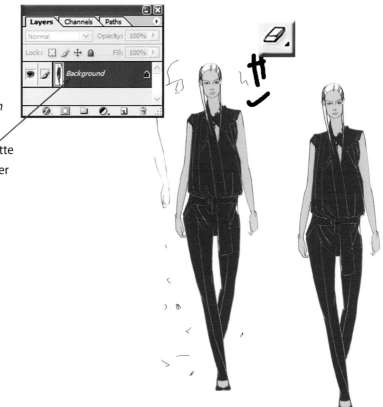

9. filters

Filters are used to add creative or dramatic effects to images and selections e.g. sharpen an image, distort, add textural effects or create dramatic changes such as making an image look like an impressionist painting, charcoal or pastel drawing. There are a large number of filters which are well worth experimenting with, a couple of which will be explained here.

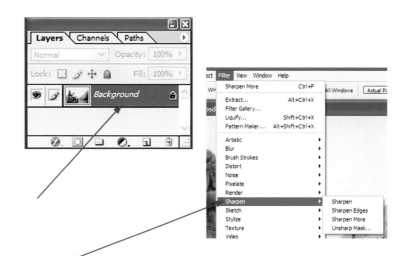

Exercise 9a: *Sharpen a scanned photograph.*

When an image is scanned, rotated, resampled, the resolution changed, or the image converted from RGB to CMYK, it may become blurred. The 'Sharpen' filters enhance and sharpen images. You can sharpen a complete image, or a selection of an image. Sharpen images once you have finished editing them e.g. once a design presentation is complete.

- Open a scanned photograph
- Select the layer to which to apply the filter (here the background layer is the only layer)
- Choose Filter (Menu Bar)>Sharpen>Sharpen ('Sharpen Edges' and 'Sharpen More' can be selected but be careful of over sharpening as the image can become grainy).

Exercise 9b: *Sharpen a scanned fashion illustration.*

- Open a scanned fashion illustration
- Repeat as above

The 'Unsharp Mask' filter gives greater control over sharpening - professionals use this for printing high resolution images - see the Help menu for more information.

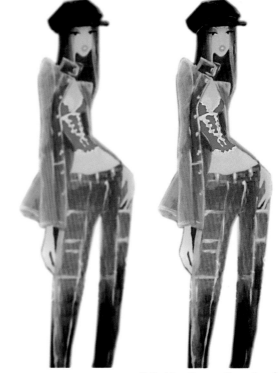

Exercise 9c: *Create a draped look to a garment.*

To create a draped look to a garment to simulate movement, the selections must first be 'filled' with a pattern and then the 'Twirl' filter can be applied.

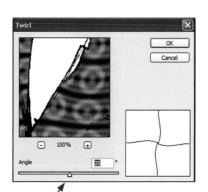

 - Select the area(s) of the garment to be filled with pattern and to which the filter is to be added (the Magic Wand tool was used here)

- 'Fill' with a pattern (see exercise 5b)

- With the selection still active, choose Filter (Menu Bar)>Distort>Twirl (to display the Twirl box)

- Enter a value in the Angle indicator (25 was entered here). To avoid 'Twirling' too much, enter a low value - check the effect in the Preview box

- Click OK

- Repeat selections until the garment is complete

- Deselect to finish.

Make selections carefully, e.g. in this example, the arms and a hand are situated in the middle of the garment. If every section of the garment had been selected at the same time, the hand would also have been twirled. Therefore, to prevent this, the top half, then the lower half, were selected and twirled separately.

The top half of the illustration is selected, Filled and Twirled

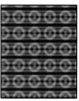

Pattern sample, used as Fill

The lower half of the illustration is selected, Filled and Twirled

Exercise 9d: *Experiment with filters and image color effects.*

This section demonstrates several more of the multitude of effects you can create to enhance your digital photographs, illustrations and presentations. Apply these effects to the entire image, a selection or a layer.

*Camera shot taken in a photographic studio by photographer **Michael Ng** for **World** clothing*

Choose Image (Menu Bar)>Adjustments> Color Balance (to display the Color Balance dialog box), and adjust the color sliders as required

Choose Image (Menu Bar)>Adjustments> Invert (to create a positive/negative effect)

Choose Filter (Menu Bar)>Artistic>Neon Glow

Choose Filter (Menu Bar)>Artistic>Colored Pencil

Filters cannot be applied to a Bitmap, and some filters are not available in CMYK mode. Work in RGB and then convert to CMYK if you need to.

© Fashion Computing - Sandra Burke

10. create and edit type

The Type Tool is used to create and edit type. Type is automatically created on its own layer. By selecting the layer you make it active and the type can then be edited. You can create a variety of effects and stylize type for presentations. (Most of the techniques here can also be used for your images.)

Exercise 10a: *Create type.*

- Select the Type Tool (Toolbox)
- The Options Bar displays the type options for formatting the text, click on the down arrows to select a font, style size etc.; click the color swatch to select a color for the type (Photoshop's default is the foreground color, black)
- Click on the image area to position the type
- Type the desired text (in this case Fabric)
- Click the 'Check/Tick' (Options Bar) when finished

- Select the Move Tool (Toolbox) to move the text on its layer
• To edit the type, the Type layer must be active (selected), then select the Type Tool, click and drag to select the type - now the type can be edited.

- Select the Vertical Type Tool to create vertical type.

Exercise 10b: *Create type in a bounding box.*

Create type in a bounding box if you have a lot of type which needs to be constrained and wrapped e.g. when describing a design.

- Select the Type Tool
- Click and drag on the image area (this defines a bounding box), as you type the text automatically wraps within the box (press Enter/return to create a line break).
- Click and drag the handles of the bounding box to change its dimensions
- Select Window (Menu Bar)>Paragraph (to display the Paragraph palette, or Character to display the Character palette), and edit the type.

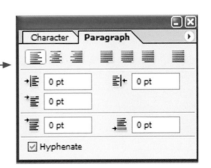

© Fashion Computing - Sandra Burke

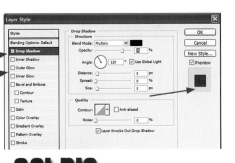

Exercise 10c: *Create a drop shadow, an inner glow, and warp type.*

- Select the Type layer in the Layers palette
- To create a drop shadow: Choose Layer (Menu Bar)>Layer Style>
Drop Shadow (the Layer Style dialog box appears), select from the
options, click OK.
- To create the inner glow: Choose Layer (Menu Bar)>Layer Style>
Inner Glow (select from the options in the Layer Style dialog box),
click OK.

 - To create the warp feature: Click on the Create warped
text (Options Bar), click on the Style box and select a style
from the drop down menu.

Exercise 10d: *Change the opacity of type.*

- Select the Type layer, and in the Layers palette reduce the
Opacity (here 70% was used - to show the effect the type was
created over another image layer).
• Opacity can also be used on images

Exercise 10e: *Rasterize and apply a filter to type.*

To apply a filter (fill, pattern, gradient) to type you must first
rasterize it - this converts the vector type layer into a regular
Photoshop layer (note that you can no longer edit the type using
the Type Tools once it is rasterized).
- Select the Type layer
- Choose Layer (Menu Bar)>Rasterize>Type (Photoshop converts
the type layer to a regular layer)
- Choose Filter (Menu Bar)>Sketch>Note Paper (try out different
filters for more creative effects).

Exercise 10f: *Fill type with pattern.*

- Select the Type layer and rasterize the type (as above)
- Select the type (the Magic Wand was used here)
- Choose Edit (Menu Bar)>Fill (the Fill box appears)
- From the Fill box click the 'Contents/Use' arrow, choose Pattern
(the Custom Pattern box appears), click on the arrow to display the
patterns and scroll to select the pattern you previously defined in
exercise 5a.
- Click OK
- The selection will be filled with the pattern.

Exercise 10g: *Fill type with a gradient.*

- Select the Type layer and rasterize the type as above
- Follow the steps as per Filling a flat with a gradient, exercise 4a.

• *See Help (Menu Bar) for more information on Type.*

11. create layer styles

You can create interesting effects to layers e.g. soft shadows, outer glow and well as color effects.

 You cannot apply a Layer Style to a Background layer. If your image only has one layer, create a duplicate of the background.

- Choose Window (Menu Bar)>Layers (to display the Layers palette), select the Background layer in the Layers palette, click on the upper right arrow (to display the Layer options) and click on Duplicate Layer.

Exercise 11: *Create a Color Overlay on a flat.*

Open your image and choose Window (Menu Bar)>Layers (to display the Layers palette if not already open)
- Click on the image Layer in the Layers palette to select it and make it active
- Choose Layer (Menu Bar)>Layer Style> Blending Options (to display the Layer Style dialog box) and choose Color Overlay
- Click on the color box (to display the Color picker box), select a color, click OK (red and green were used here), change the opacity (50% was used here), click OK
- The image (jacket) will now have an overlay of color.

 If you need to redefine the design lines of the flat (in this case the black in the print as well as the design lines) use the Color Range Command (Photoshop Essential Techniques, exercise 8d) to select the dull/black areas of the flat, and Fill with black (exercise 3a.), or choose Image (Menu Bar)>Adjustments and change Brightness etc.

You are encouraged to experiment with more tools and techniques such as Layer Masks, Color Adjustments and drawing paths using the Pen Tool. Use your 'Help' (Menu Bar) for more information.

Graphics Drawing software is used together with Photoshop to further develop designs and presentations, for example, flats which are created in Illustrator, CorelDRAW or Freehand, can be placed and edited in Photoshop to create dynamic design presentations.

Shortcut Tips

To Zoom using shortcut keys when you are working with any tool:

PC zoom in: Press Ctrl + space bar

PC zoom in: Press Ctrl + space bar + alt

Mac zoom in: Press Apple + space bar

Mac zoom out: Press Apple + space bar + option

Hand Tool: When working in either platform and any tool, press the space bar to give you the Hand Tool.

Shirt - a selection was made with the Polygon Lasso Tool on its own Shirt layer, then filled with pattern and Opacity set to 50%

This chapter has explained how to use 11 key image editing techniques, tools and commands to create color and effects. These skills, including the skills learnt in the previous chapter, *Photoshop Essential Tools,* form the foundation for the following chapter, *Design Presentations.*

A line drawing of a fashion model was scanned, the Pattern defined, the line drawing selected and filled with the Pattern

*An **instructor's manual** with exercises will be available for lecturers, see www.knowledgezone.net*

11
design presentations

Fashion Illustration by **Alissa Stytsenko-Berdnik**
Ink on paper, scanned illustration and fabric swatch,
edited in Illustrator and Photoshop

Design Presentations, also called Storyboards, are the fashion designers' creative format to communicate clothing designs and concepts to the design team, buyers, merchandisers, and marketing teams. These design presentations include;

- Design Concepts - themes, concepts and mood boards
- Fashion Design boards - clothing ranges or collections for the forthcoming season
- Fabric and Color - the fabric and color palettes or colorways for the collection
- Trend Forecasting - directional looks and future trends.
- Promotional Artwork, Brochures and Advertisements - for media and magazines.

A design presentation can be hand drawn and/or computer generated and could include the following components:

- Designs illustrated on the fashion figure
- Designs drawn as flats/working drawings
- Fabric swatches, color story, trims
- Photographic images, graphics and magazine pictures (tear sheets or swipes).

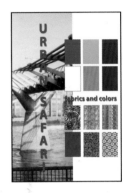

This chapter explains how to use Photoshop to create professional design presentations by applying the 21 key image editing techniques which were introduced in the previous chapters, Chapter 9, *Photoshop Essential Tools*, and Chapter 10, *Photoshop Color and Effects*. Figure 11.1 presents an overview of these presentations, and outlines the structure of this chapter.

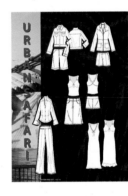

presentation	name	exercises include
1. Design Concept	Urban Safari 1	A scanned fashion illustration, a photograph for the background, and digital type
2. Fabric and Color	Urban Safari 2	Scanned fabric swatches, a photograph for the background, and digital type
3. Fashion Design - Flats (scanned)	Urban Safari 3	Scanned flats, a photograph for the background, and digital type
4. Fashion Design - Fashion Illustration	Couture Rebel	Scanned fashion illustrations (to be 'filled' in Photoshop), a scanned fabric for the background, and digital type
5. Fashion and Fabric Design	Pearl Rock	A digital fabric design and flats, and a digital or scanned photograph
6. Gallery of Design Presentations	Contributing Designers and Illustrators	Design work (flats, presentations, fashion illustrations and fabric designs) from designers and illustrators displaying a variety of computer techniques

Figure 11.1
Table of Photoshop presentations and exercises

8 hot tips

 Save your file at regular intervals, 5-10 minutes.

 Do a 'Save As' under a different name as you build up your job so that you can revert to that copy if something goes 'horribly wrong' or you do not like the way your latest presentation looks.

 Name each Layer so that you can recognise them instantly. This is especially useful when creating complex presentations with many layers (see Photoshop Essential Tools, exercise 9ii).

 Use the History palette, undo or revert to return an image to a previous state (see Photoshop Essential Tools, exercise 7).

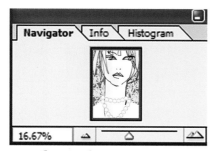

 Use the Navigator palette, Hand Tool, Zoom Tool and scroll bars to work around the active image area (see Photoshop Essential Tools, exercise 3).

 Minimizing and moving palettes is useful to clean up the work area and see the images without excess clutter.

 Use the Sharpen Filter with caution (see Photoshop Color and Effects, exercise 9a and 9b).

 Presentations can also be created in graphics drawing programs, Illustrator, CorelDRAW or Freehand, but Photoshop tends to allow greater flexibility to create more dynamic presentations especially when working with scanned images and photographs.

Fashion Illustration, Elle by **Stuart McKenzie**
Ink on paper, scanned illustration and fabric swatch, edited in Photoshop

creating design presentations

When you create a design presentation, it is important to have a target size and resolution for the intended output of the presentation, (refer *Scanning and Digital Photography*, step 3, and *Computer Basics,* Resolution). Use 72 dpi for the Internet, 200 dpi for most printers, 300 dpi for commercial printing.

The Design Presentations in these exercises are created using the following steps:

step 1 - create a folder for the presentation
- Create a folder and move or copy all the image files for the presentation into the folder e.g. scanned flats, fashion illustrations and fabrics, digital photographs, computer generated flats.

UrbanSafari1_Presentation1

step 2 - create a new file for the presentation
- Create and save a new file (.psd), see *Photoshop Essential Tools,* exercise 1. This is the layout (active image area) where the presentation is created. All the images for the presentation will be added to this new blank layout.

step 3 - edit and move images
- Edit each image ('Fill' with pattern, crop, adjust colors), then select and drag/copy to the layout.
(You can also edit an image within the layout itself - select the image's layer in the Layers palette, e.g. move the image around the presentation, set blending modes, erase parts of the image that are not needed, move the image in front or behind another image by moving the image layer above or below another layer, set blending modes, and adjust colors.)

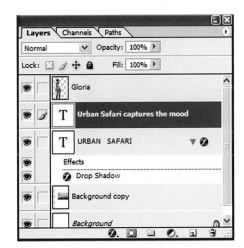

step 4 - create type
Create, edit and manipulate type for the presentation.

step 5 - save, flatten, sharpen
When the design presentation is complete, save the file in the appropriate format for the output (for print or screen), flatten (see *Computer Basics,* Layers) and sharpen (see *Photoshop Color and Effects,* exercise 9a and 9b).

When working with multiple layers it is useful to turn off the 'non active' layers by clicking on the 'Eye' icon next to the image in the Layers palette - this allows you to focus on the 'active' image.

All the exercises in the following Design Presentation worked examples are explained in Chapter 9, Photoshop Essential Tools, and Chapter 10, Photoshop Color and Effects.

URBAN SAFARI

Urban Safari captures the mood of vibrant diversity, from city living to a land of wild animals with a touch of femininity - cityscape, rebel spirit and couture mixed with rock attitude.

Colors: Sunset Red, Merlot Red, Camel, Khaki, Black, White and Denim Blue

Fabrics: Silky lingerie fabrics meet sports cottons, high tech fabrics, denim and lace

Prints: 60s Floral, Stripes, Snake and Zebra Animal Prints

presentation 1 - **design concept/theme**

This first worked example, Urban Safari 1, is a design concept/mood presentation.

UrbanSafari1_Presentation1

step 1 - create a folder for the presentation

- Create a folder (this example is named *UrbanSafari1_Presention1*) and copy all the image files for this presentation into the folder, these include;

- A scanned photograph (this example is the 'Millennium' walking bridge in London which I shot during one of my fashion research trips. The bridge adds to the mood for the 'Urban' theme)

- A scanned fashion illustration rendered/filled with color (the fashion illustration used here expresses both the Urban and Safari theme).

step 2 - create a new file for the presentation

- Create a new file (this file is saved as *UrbanSafari1_Concept*).

step 3 - edit and move images

- First image: Open the scanned photograph (bridge) and edit as required (here the yellow sign at the bottom of the photograph was selected and filled with a more subtle color, and the image cropped and the canvas size increased at the top of the photograph)
- Select the image, choose Select (Menu Bar)>All, then select the Move Tool and drag the selection to copy it on to the layout.

- Second Image: Open the fashion illustration image and edit as required (here the scarf, body of the bag, and front inset of the shoes were selected using the Magic Wand, and 'Filled' with 'Pattern')
- Select the image using the Magic Wand Tool to select the background, then choose Select (Menu Bar)>Inverse (to select the fashion illustration)
- Select the Move Tool, drag the selection to copy it on to the layout.

step 4 - create type

- Vertical Type: Select the Vertical Type Tool, select the Font family, font type, font size and text color (Myriad Pro, Bold, 60pt, neutral was used here) and type the theme e.g. *URBAN SAFARI*
- Drop Shadow: Choose Layer (Menu Bar)>Layer Style>Drop Shadow (use the default setting, or adjust the values and color).
- Descriptive text: Select the Type Tool, click on the image and drag to create the bounding box, select the Font family, font type, font size and text color (Myriad Pro, Regular, 24pt, red).

Urban Safari captures the mood of vibrant diversity, from city living to a land of wild

step 5 - save, flatten, sharpen

- Save in the appropriate format for the output (for print or screen), flatten and sharpen (*Computer Basics* and *Photoshop - Color and Effects* chapters).

URBAN SAFARI

fabrics and colors

presentation 2 - **fabric and colors**

This second worked example, *Urban Safari 2* is a fabric and color presentation and displays the fabrics and colors used in the collection.

step 1 - create a folder for the presentation
- Create a folder (this example is called *UrbanSafari2_ Presentation2)* and copy all the image files for this presentation into the folder, these include;
- • A scanned photograph (the portrait view of the Millennium bridge was scanned at 400%, grayscale - this image enhances the Urban theme and, being in grayscale, the image will not overpower the fabrics)
- • Scanned Fabric swatches (these fabrics were sourced from fabric suppliers, and scanned at 50% - the fabrics were chosen as they work well together as a range, and are suitable for the target market and style of clothing).

step 2 - create a new file for the presentation
- Create a new file (this file was saved as *UrbanSafari2_Fabrics).*

step 3 - edit and move images
- First image: Open the photograph for the background image (bridge), and crop to the required size using the Crop Tool (here the left side of the photograph was cropped to achieve a slim portrait view)
- Select the image, choose Select (Menu Bar)>All, then select the Move Tool and drag the selection to copy it on to the layout.

- Fabric Swatches: Open a fabric image, select the Rectangular Marquee Tool, on the Options Bar set values; Fixed Size, width 4cms, height 6cms
- Select the Move tool and drag the fabric selection to copy it on to the layout
- Repeat the technique until all the fabric swatches are copied on to the layout.

step 4 - create type
- Vertical Type 'URBAN SAFARI' - create as per Design Presentation 1 but in red and larger font size
- Horizontal type 'Fabrics and Colors' - select the Type Tool, select the Font family, font type, font size and text color (Myriad Pro, Bold, 48pt, red was used here), and type Fabrics and Colours.

step 5 - save, flatten, sharpen
- Save in the appropriate format for the output (for print or screen), flatten and sharpen.

UrbanSafari 2_Presentation 2

fabrics and colors

In the Layers palette the Type layers are easily recognised as they automatically take on the first words of the text as the Layer name.

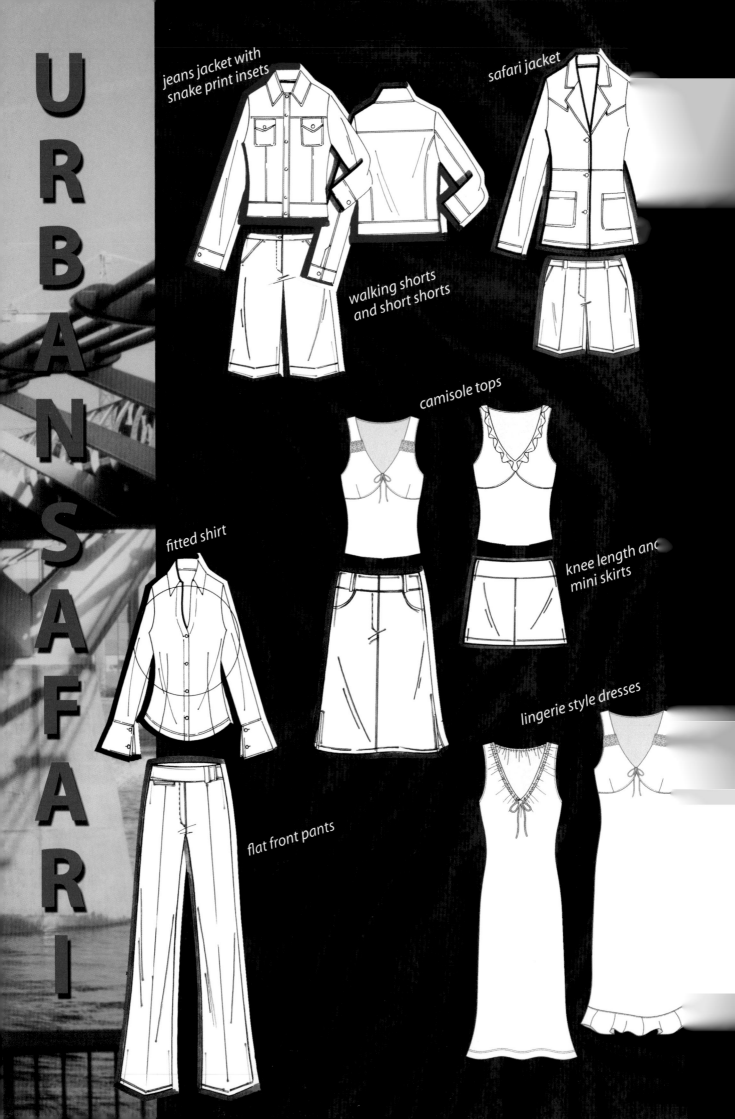

URBAN SAFARI

jeans jacket with snake print insets

safari jacket

walking shorts and short shorts

camisole tops

fitted shirt

knee length and mini skirts

lingerie style dresses

flat front pants

presentation 3 - **fashion design presentation**

This third example, *Urban Safari 3* is a fashion design presentation displaying the scanned flats for the collection.

UrbanSafari 3_FlatsPresentation3

step 1 - **create a folder for the presentation**

- Create a folder *(UrbanSafari3_ Flats Presentation3)* and copy all the image files for this presentation into the folder, these include;
   • A scanned fabric for the background (the Zebra print was scanned 100%)
   • A scanned photograph (the bridge as per Design Presentation 2).
   • Scanned hand drawn flats (these flats were scanned at 100%, and present a small, capsule collection suitable for the fabrics).

step 2 - **create a new file for the layout**

- Create a new file (this file was saved as *UrbanSafari3_Flats,* and created with a black background).

step 3 - **edit and move images**

- First image: Open the scanned fabric (Zebra print), select using Select (Menu Bar)>All, then select the Move Tool and drag the selection to copy it on to the layout
- In the Layers palette, click on the print layer (Zebra print) to make it active. Choose Layer (Menu Bar) Layers>Layer Style>Blending Options (to display the Layer Style dialog box) and choose Color Overlay (purple, and 25% opacity was used here) - this forms a color overlay on the print and reduces the definition of the pattern so that it does become the focus of the presentation (*Photoshop Color and Effects,* exercise 11).

- Second image: Open the photograph (bridge) image, edit, crop as desired, then select as per Design Presentation 2, add a Color Overlay as above but use 20% opacity
- Select the Move Tool and drag the selection to copy it on to the layout

- Flats: Open a flat, select the background using the Magic Wand Tool, and then choose Select (Menu Bar)>Inverse to select the flat
- Select the Move Tool and drag the selection to copy it on to the layout
- Repeat the technique until all the flats are copied on to the layout
   • To reposition a flat, select its layer and move it with the Move Tool e.g. you may wish to group the flats or slightly overlap them.

step 4 - **create type**

- URBAN SAFARI vertical type - create as per Design Presentation 2
- Descriptive text: Select the Type Tool, select the Font, type, size, color (Myriad Pro, Italic, 18, white was used here), type a description for each flat (this creates a new type layer each time)
- Select the Move Tool, choose Edit (Menu Bar)>Transform>Rotate, to rotate each text layer as desired.

step 5 - **save, flatten, sharpen**

- Save in the appropriate format for the output (for print or screen), flatten and sharpen (*Computer Basics* and *Photoshop - Color and Effects* chapters).

jeans jacket with snake print insets

© Fashion Computing - Sandra Burke

COUTURE REBEL

Soft relaxed and sexy styling
An eclectic mix of couture and the pirate
rebel within oneself
Pirate garments of vests, soft trousers and
flowing tops, skirts and dresses
Couture fabrics of silk and georgette
Rebel prints of camouflage flowers
Pirate accessories of strappy leather belts
slung across the body in white or brown
leather

presentation 4 - **fashion design (illustration) presentation**

This fourth worked example, *Couture Rebel,* is a fashion design presentation displaying the collection as a fashion illustration.

step 1 - create a folder for the presentation

- Create a folder (*CoutureRebel_Presentation4)* and copy all the image files for this presentation into the folder, these include;
  - Scanned fabric
  - Scanned line art (fashion illustrations) - scanned at 100% and filled in Photoshop.

📁 CoutureRebel_Presentation4

step 2 - create a new file for the presentation

- Create a new file (this file is saved as *Couture Rebel).*

step 3 - edit and move images

- First image: Open the image of the fabric for the background (Camouflage Floral print)
- In the Layers palette, click on the print layer to make it active, add a Color Overlay as per Presentation 3, step 3 (khaki, and 35% opacity was used here)
- Select the image, choose Select (Menu Bar)>All, then select the Move Tool and drag the selection to copy it on to the layout

- Fashion images: Open a fashion illustration, select the individual areas (flesh, clothing, hair etc.) and fill with color and/or pattern
- Select the background using the Magic Wand Tool, and then choose Select (Menu Bar)>Inverse (to select the illustration)
- Select the Move Tool and drag the selection to copy it on to the layout
- To edit the size of an illustration; select the fashion illustration's layer in the Layer palette, choose Edit (Menu Bar)>Transform>Scale (see *Photoshop Essential Tools,* exercise 10)
- Repeat the technique until all the fashion illustrations are copied on to the layout
- To reposition an illustration, select its layer and move it with the Move Tool e.g. you may wish to group the illustration or slightly overlap them.

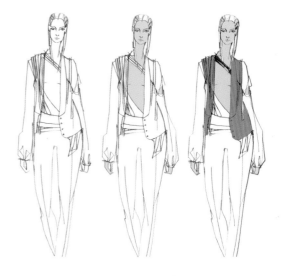

step 4 - create type

- COUTURE REBEL text: Select the Type Tool, click on the image and drag to create the bounding box, select the Font family, font type, font size and text color (Myriad Pro, Regular, 60pt and 24pt, black was used here). (For the text to stand out against the printed background a rectangle was drawn using the Rectangle Tool, filled with color and no stroke, the layer dragged below the Text layer).

step 5 - save, flatten, sharpen

- Save in the appropriate format for the output (for print or screen), flatten and sharpen).

COUTURE REBEL

Soft relaxed and sexy styling
An eclectic mix of couture and the pirate rebel within oneself
Pirate garments of vests, soft trousers and flowing tops, skirts and dresses
Couture fabrics of silk and georgette
Rebel prints of camouflage flowers
Pirate accessories of strappy leather belts slung across the body in white or brown leather

Pearls print and Bird print by **Christopher Davies** *for* **World** *clothing*
Pencil on paper, edited in Illustrator and Photoshop
Photographer **Michael NG**

presentation 5 - **fashion and fabric design presentation**

This fifth worked example, *Pearl Rock,* is a fashion and fabric design presentation.

step 1 - create a folder for the presentation

- Create a folder (*PearlRock_Presentation 6)* and copy all the image files for this presentation into the folder, these include;
• Fabric design (this Pearls print was created by hand and edited in Illustrator)
• Photograph of a model wearing the fashion designs (digital or scanned)
• Computer generated flats (these flats were created in Illustrator and filled with color and pattern in Photoshop)
• Fabric print (the Bird screen print was sketched by hand and edited in Illustrator).

step 2 - create a new file for the presentation

- Create a new file (this file is saved as *Pearl Rock).*

step 3 - edit and move

- First image: Open the image of the fabric print
- Select the image, choose Select (Menu Bar)>All, then select the Move Tool and drag the selection to copy it on to the layout

 - Second image: Open the photograph of the model, crop using the Crop Tool as required (the background was cropped here to focus on the model)
- Select (Menu Bar)>All, select the Move Tool and drag the selection to copy it on to the layout, and rotate to position, choose Edit (Menu Bar)>Transform> Rotate

- Flats: Open a flat; select and fill with color
- Select the background using the Magic Wand Tool, and then choose Select (Menu Bar)>Inverse (to select the flat)
- Select the Move Tool and drag the selection to copy it on to the layout
- Repeat the technique until all the flats are copied on to the layout
  • The tank top with the *Bird* screen print: The *Bird* print EPS file was opened (the EPS file had been saved with a transparent background), the print was selected and, with the Move Tool, was dragged to the top and positioned. The print was too big for the top so was scaled in the Layers Palette, using Edit (Menu Bar)>Transform>Scale (see *Photoshop Essential Tools,* exercise 10)
  • The skirt with the Pearls print basque: The Pearls print was opened, the pattern was defined and the basque of the skirt was filled with the pattern (see *Photoshop Color and Effects,* exercise 5 to 'Define' and 'Fill'). Select the Magic Wand Tool to select the basque, choose Edit (Menu Bar)>Fill and choose the *Pearls* pattern

- **Rotate the flats:** Select the skirt layer, choose Edit (Menu Bar)>Transform> Rotate (to rotate the top on the presentation; repeat procedure for the top)
- **Stroke line around the flats:** Select the flat layer, add a stroke line (see *Photoshop Color and Effects,* exercise 7). Repeat the technique for all flats - they will stand out from the background (white, 20pt, center, was used here)

step 5 - save, flatten, sharpen

- Save in the appropriate format for the output (for print or screen), flatten and sharpen.

Take photographs of your clothing on a model or a mannequin and combine it with flats and fabrics to create an interesting presentation.

📁 PearlRock_Presentation5

To color 'Fill' the print of the skirt basque, the white background of the Pearl print was selected using Color Range and then filled with color.

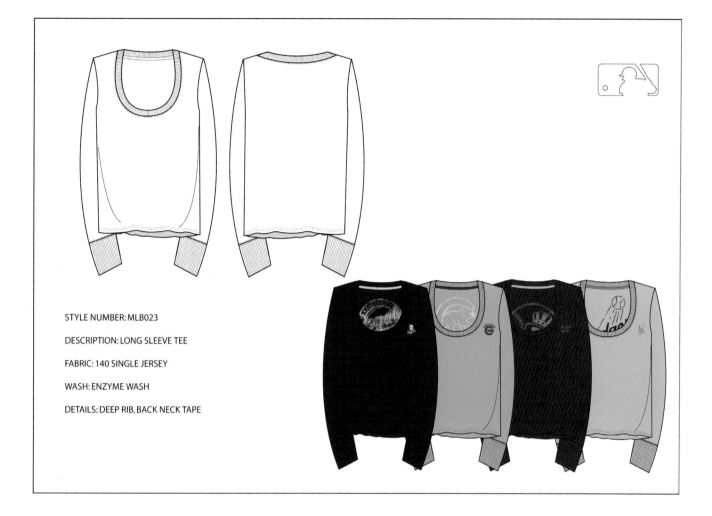

STYLE NUMBER: MLB023

DESCRIPTION: LONG SLEEVE TEE

FABRIC: 140 SINGLE JERSEY

WASH: ENZYME WASH

DETAILS: DEEP RIB, BACK NECK TAPE

Fashion Design Presentation by **Bureaux Design**, London

Womenswear range of jersey tops designed for major league baseball

Flats presentation, flats drawn and filled in Illustrator and graphics
created in Photoshop

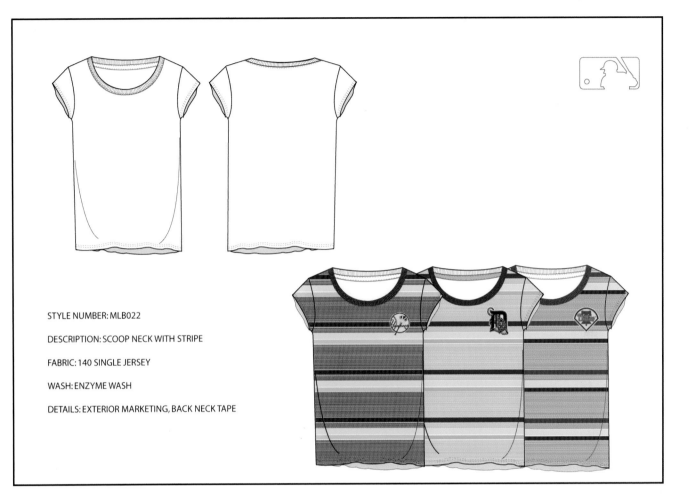

STYLE NUMBER: MLB022

DESCRIPTION: SCOOP NECK WITH STRIPE

FABRIC: 140 SINGLE JERSEY

WASH: ENZYME WASH

DETAILS: EXTERIOR MARKETING, BACK NECK TAPE

Fashion Design Presentation by **Bureaux Design,** London

Womenswear range of jersey tops designed for major league baseball

Flats presentation, flats drawn and filled in Illustrator and graphics
created in Photoshop

Fashion Design Presentation Series created by **Alissa Stytsenko-Berdnik,** fashion designer and illustrator, <www.alissa.co.nz>

Ink on paper, scanned illustration and fabrics, edited in Illustrator and Photoshop

Fashion Design Presentation Series created by **Alissa Stytsenko-Berdnik,** fashion designer and illustrator, <www.alissa.co.nz>

Ink on paper, scanned illustrations and fabrics, edited in Illustrator and Photoshop

Fashion Illustration, *Esquire* by **Stuart McKenzie,** fashion illustrator, London

Ink on paper, scanned illustration and fabrics, edited in Photoshop

Fashion Illustrations by **Stuart McKenzie,**
fashion illustrator, London

Ink on paper, scanned illustration and
fabrics, edited in Photoshop

Fashion Design Presentation Series created by **Frances Howie,** Fashion Designer, Lanvin, Paris

Ink on paper, scanned illustrations and fabrics, digital photographs, edited in Illustrator and Photoshop

The final shapes will emerge in several different ways:
i. during the toiling process, while the shadows are wrapped/strapped onto the three dimensional
ii. as an OHP projection falls on the stand in a darkened room

Fashion Design Presentation Series created by **Frances Howie,** Fashion Designer, Lanvin, Paris

Ink on paper, scanned illustrations and fabrics, digital photographs, edited in Illustrator and Photoshop

Fashion Design Presentation Series created by **Frances Howie,** Fashion Designer, Lanvin, Paris

Ink on paper, scanned illustrations and fabrics, digital photographs, edited in Illustrator and Photoshop

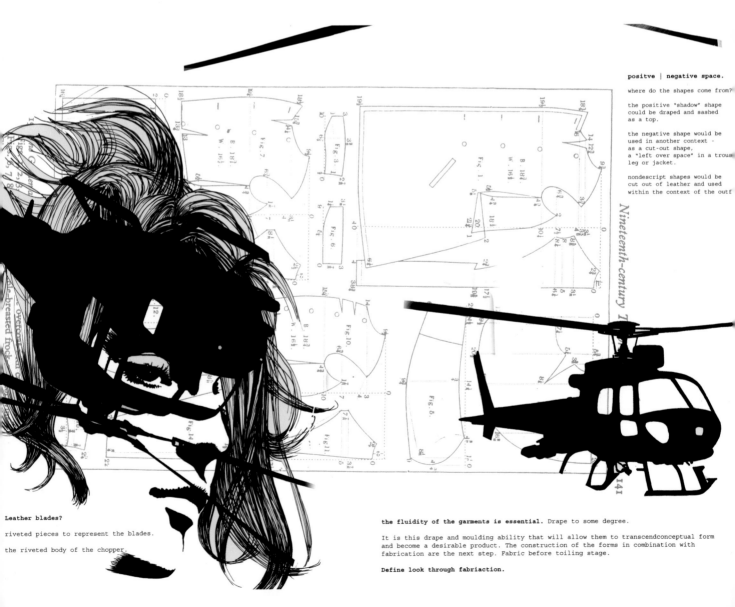

positve | negative space.

where do the shapes come from?

the positive "shadow" shape could be draped and sashed as a top.

the negative shape would be used in another context - as a cut-out shape, a "left over space" in a trous leg or jacket.

nondescript shapes would be cut out of leather and used within the context of the outf

Leather blades?

riveted pieces to represent the blades.

the riveted body of the chopper.

the fluidity of the garments is essential. Drape to some degree.

It is this drape and moulding ability that will allow them to transcendconceptual form and become a desirable product. The construction of the forms in combination with fabrication are the next step. Fabric before toiling stage.

Define look through fabriaction.

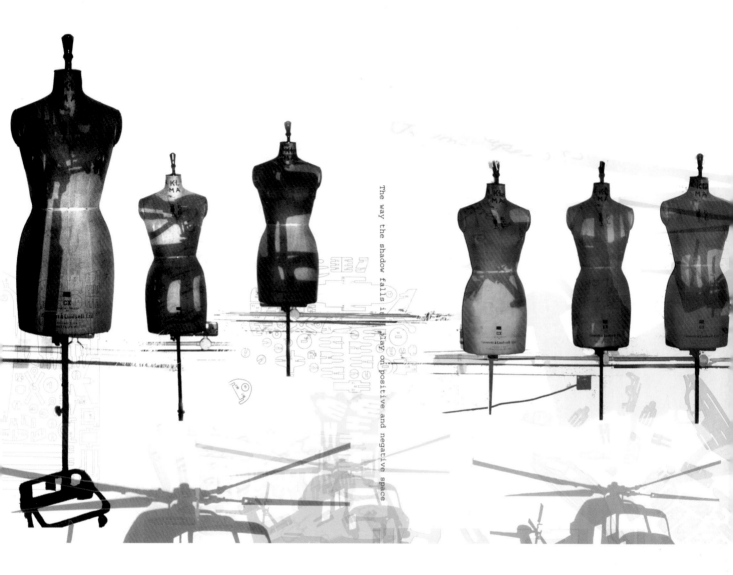

The way the shadow falls is a play on positive and negative space

Fashion Design Presentation Series created by **Frances Howie,** Fashion Designer, Lanvin, Paris

Ink on paper, scanned illustrations and fabrics, digital photographs, edited in Illustrator and Photoshop

2. Paper Aviary

Bird Print Theme by **Christopher Davies** for *World* clothing
Pencil on paper, edited in Illustrator and Photoshop
(Fashion Illustration by France Howie, edited in Photoshop)

Bird Print Theme, screen print by **Christopher Davies** for **World** clothing

Pencil on paper, edited in Illustrator and Photoshop, and screen print, gold metallic print on black satin

jonathan kyle farmer ma (rca) – fashion designer/illustrator

Fashion Illustrations by **Jonathan Kyle Farmer,** ma (rca),
Fashion Designer and Illustrator

Ink, Pantone and acrylic on paper, scanned illustrations
and fabrics, edited in Illustrator and Photoshop

SPORTMAX

Fashion Illustrations by **Jonathan Kyle Farmer,** ma (rca), Fashion Designer and Illustrator

Ink on paper, collage, applique, scanned illustrations and fabrics, edited in Illustrator and Photoshop

'Black Sabbath' (opposite page) and 'Desdemona' (this page) by **Lynnette Cook,** Fashion Illustrator, London

Ink on paper, scanned illustrations, filled with color and gradients in CorelDRAW

This chapter has explained how to create professional design presentations by applying Photoshop's key image editing techniques. It has also brought together the skills learnt in all the previous chapters, drawing techniques, creating flats, scanning and digital photography.

The following chapter, *Digital Design Portfolio*, will discuss how these design presentations can be collated to create a digital portfolio, the passport to your career.

An ***instructor's manual*** *with exercises will be available for lecturers, see www.knowledgezone.net*

12

digital
portfolio

Fashion Illustration by **Alissa Stytsenko-Berdnik**
Ink on paper, scanned illustration and fabric swatch, edited in Illustrator and Photoshop

design portfolio

Your fashion design portfolio is not just a collection of your work and an example of your talent, it is also your **principle marketing tool.** A creative and well planned portfolio provides visual evidence of your capabilities and your unique qualities. It is a means to express your range of demonstrable skills and your fashion design expertise - your fashion drawing, illustration and presentation skills, plus technical ability (pattern making and garment construction). Your portfolio should be constantly updated - it is your passport to success and career development.

In *Fashion Artist* I explained how to create a design portfolio using hand drawn, and cut and paste techniques. This chapter will discuss how technology can be used to create a digital design portfolio using PowerPoint.

Your digital portfolio can be presented to a live audience, saved as a slide show and run on any computer, sent as an email attachment and also published on the Internet. With the rapid development of computer technology, companies are increasingly using the Internet (websites, email, web conferencing etc.) as their means of visual communication. Once you create a digital portfolio you will be able to present your work to anyone anywhere in the world with the push of a button.

The confines of this book only allow for a brief overview of the key points. For more information also see the 'Help' (Menu Bar); go online and connect to *www.microsoft.com* where you will find free tutorials and tips for PowerPoint, FrontPage, websites and lots more; see *Further Reading* at the end of *Fashion Computing.*

plan your digital design portfolio

When creating your digital design portfolio you should plan the contents of the layout carefully to keep the presentation short, sharp and interesting to retain the attention and interest of the viewer or audience. Approximately, 20 images will adequately demonstrate your creative skills, and the text should be kept to a minimum.

- **Introduction:** Start with something about yourself; unique to you, perhaps a logo or graphic. Include your details (name, address, email, website address, content)
- **Variety:** Display your creative talents and design skills by presenting a range of artwork to keep the portfolio exciting and informative
- **Design Sense:** Keep your portfolio creative and graphically well presented, not necessarily wild on every page, but showing good design sense and strong themes
- **Layout:** Organise your portfolio either by design or season (latest first) and finish with a dynamic finale (wedding, evening wear).

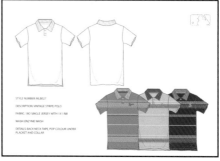

For more information see *Fashion Artist - Drawing Techniques to Portfolio Presentation.*

create a powerpoint presentation

To create a PowerPoint design presentation you simply create a series of slide images of your artwork and add any necessary explanatory text. Graphics created in drawing and image editing programs, including scanned and digital photographs can be inserted into a PowerPoint presentation. You can insert bitmap or vector images, color and grayscale. The most popular graphic formats to use are JPG, GIF and BMP, but PowerPoint will also accept TIFF, EPS, WMF etc. Special effects (transitions), music, movies and animation can be included but these should be used sparingly as they can distract from the impact of the presentation.

step 1 - create folder for the presentation

- Create a folder and copy the all image files for the presentation into the folder (this example is saved as *PPt_Design_Portfolio*):

- It is a good idea to have a target size and resolution in mind for the intended output of the presentation (refer *Scanning and Digital Photography* chapter and *Computer Basics*).

- 96 dpi for web/screen

- 200 dpi for print

- Image size of 800x600 pixels

By choosing the correct resolution for the images, and scaling and sampling the images before inserting them into PowerPoint (see *Photoshop - Colour and Effects*), will make the images easier to manipulate - for further adjustments you can also compress and scale the image within the slide.

step 2 - create a new blank presentation

- In PowerPoint choose File (Menu Bar)>New Presentation (to display a new blank presentation).

• You can also select from the AutoContent Wizard or Design Templates and choose one of PowerPoint's existing layouts.

• If you intend to insert visuals rather than text and graphs it is best to choose the blank presentation.

- To change the slide to portrait view choose File (Menu Bar)>Page Setup and select from the Page Setup box.

step 3 - add text

- Click in the text placeholders, type in the text - move and resize the placeholder.

- **Format Text:** To format text (font, size, color, align etc.), select the text, choose Format (Menu Bar) and select from the drop down menu.

PPt_Design_Portfolio

slide sorter - views

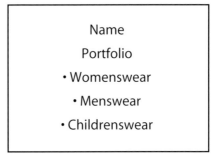

Name

Portfolio

• Womenswear

• Menswear

• Childrenswear

© Fashion Computing - Sandra Burke

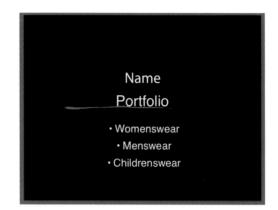

 - **Additional Text:** To create additional text in a new text box, click on the text box button in the Drawing toolbar, click and drag on the slide and add the text.

- **Bullet Points** - to create bulleted points for increased impact
- click in the relevant text box and select the text, choose Format (Menu Bar)>Bullets and Numbering.

- **Slide Design:** Choose Format (Menu Bar) and choose Slide Design, Slide Layout, Slide Color Scheme, Slide Background (to display a drop-down menu of choices, and select Apply to all slides or Apply to the current slide).

step 4 -create additional slides

- Choose Insert (Menu Bar)>New Slide.

step 5 - insert images

- **Image:** Position the insertion point at the location on the slide where you want to insert the picture, choose Insert (Menu Bar)>Picture>From File, then open the folder(s) that contains the image and select the image.

- **Compression:** If you need to compress an image within the slide, choose View (Menu Bar)>Toolbars>Picture (to display the Picture options) and select the Compress Pictures button and select from the options.

step 6 - moving slides

- To reposition a slide in Outline View or Slide View, click on a slide marker and drag it to the new position (for multiple slides, hold down Shift and click).

step 7

- Click the Slide Show icon to look at the slide.

step 8

When you save for the first time you have a choice of formats, the most common being a PowerPoint Template (.ppt). Use 'Save As' if you need to save in another format and select from the list depending on how you wish your presentation to be viewed.

 • PowerPoint Show (.pps) (slide show)

 • Save for print

 • Save for the Web or as an email attachment

 • Save on CD-ROM (to disc) and take your disc around the world
   instead of a bulky portfolio

 • Save as overheads (handouts can be printed out)

 • PDF file to be viewed on Acrobat Reader

You are now ready to get out there and show the world what you can do!!

*An **instructor's manual** with exercises will be available for lecturers, see www.knowledgezone.net*

fashion CAD

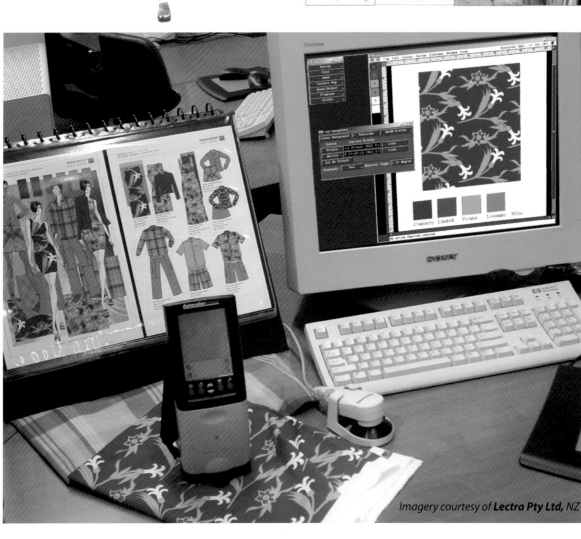

*Imagery courtesy of **Lectra Pty Ltd**, NZ*

CAD/CAM was initially developed as an interactive computer design system for the textile industry, then introduced into apparel for pattern making and grading, and more recently for fashion design.

There are a number of fashion software programs designed specifically for the small business and freelance designer (*see Computer Tool Kit*), but the larger apparel companies are more likely to use the powerful CAD Apparel and Textile Suites produced by Lectra and Gerber. These suites have been developed to integrate all areas of the apparel process from apparel and textile design, pattern making, grading, garment production through to merchandising and data management. Consequently, the suites are expensive but enable large companies to achieve economies of scale.

These giants of the apparel industry can be tailored to meet the clients' needs for any sector of their apparel businesses. For example, on the fashion design side, graphics software such CorelDRAW and Photoshop are compatible with the Gerber and Lectra systems.

The drawing and image editing skills covered in *Fashion Computing* are similar to the tools and techniques used by the more specific fashion software, Lectra and Gerber.

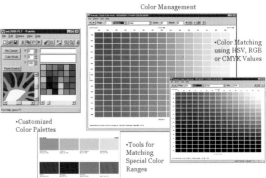

Artworks Palette & Colorbook

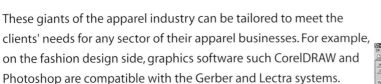

*Imagery courtesy of **Gerber (Artworks)***

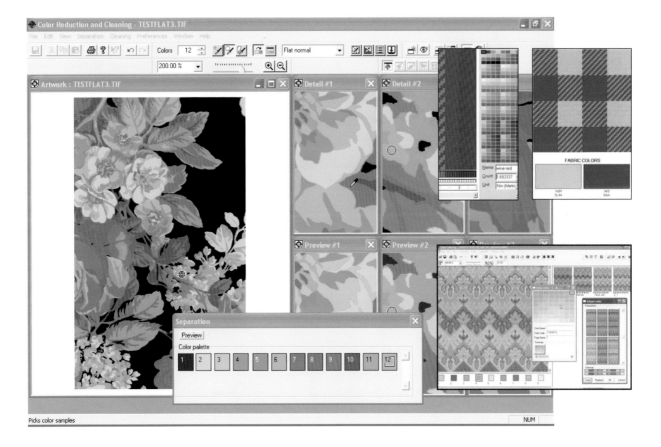

*Imagery courtesy of **Lectra Pty Ltd**, NZ*

lectra cad suite

Image, courtesy of **Lectra** PTY Ltd, NZ, shows graphically how the CAD suite has been developed to integrate all areas of the apparel process from apparel and textile design, to pattern making, grading and garment production, through to the finished product ready for dispatch. For more information visit the website <www.lectra.com>.

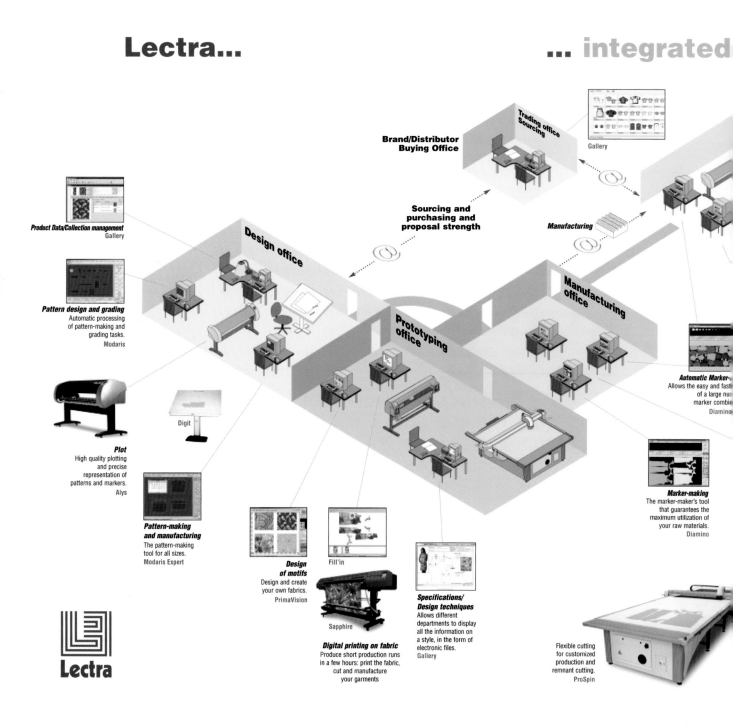

Lectra...

... integrated

Trading office
Sourcing

Brand/Distributor
Buying Office

Gallery

Product Data/Collection management
Gallery

Sourcing and
purchasing and
proposal strength

Manufacturing

Design office

Pattern design and grading
Automatic processing
of pattern-making and
grading tasks.
Modaris

Manufacturing
office

Prototyping
office

Automatic Marker-
Allows the easy and fast
of a large nu
marker combi
Diamino

Digit

Plot
High quality plotting
and precise
representation of
patterns and markers.
Alys

Marker-making
The marker-maker's tool
that guarantees the
maximum utilization of
your raw materials.
Diamino

*Pattern-making
and manufacturing*
The pattern-making
tool for all sizes.
Modaris Expert

*Design
of motifs*
Design and create
your own fabrics.
PrimaVision

Fill'in

*Specifications/
Design techniques*
Allows different
departments to display
all the information on
a style, in the form of
electronic files.
Gallery

Sapphire

Digital printing on fabric
Produce short production runs
in a few hours: print the fabric,
cut and manufacture
your garments

Flexible cutting
for customized
production and
remnant cutting.
ProSpin

Lectra

modular solutions dedicated to the Apparel industry

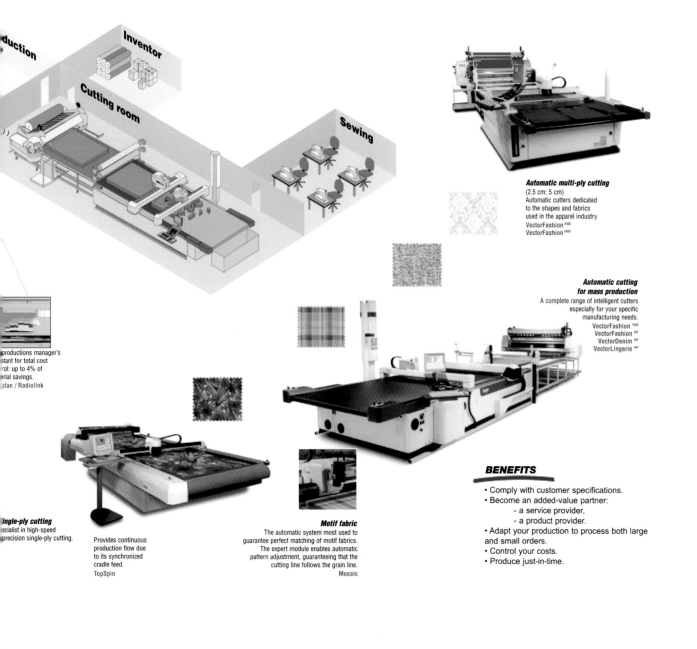

Automatic multi-ply cutting
(2.5 cm; 5 cm)
Automatic cutters dedicated
to the shapes and fabrics
used in the apparel industry
VectorFashion [7500]
VectorFashion [5000]

**Automatic cutting
for mass production**
A complete range of intelligent cutters
especially for your specific
manufacturing needs.
VectorFashion [7500]
VectorFashion [90]
VectorDenim [90]
VectorLingerie [90]

... productions manager's
...stant for total cost
...rol: up to 4% of
...erial savings.
...plan / Radiolink

...ingle-ply cutting
...ecialist in high-speed
...precision single-ply cutting.

Provides continuous
production flow due
to its synchronized
cradle feed.
TopSpin

Motif fabric
The automatic system most used to
guarantee perfect matching of motif fabrics.
The expert module enables automatic
pattern adjustment, guaranteeing that the
cutting line follows the grain line.
Mosaic

BENEFITS

- Comply with customer specifications.
- Become an added-value partner:
  - a service provider,
  - a product provider.
- Adapt your production to process both large and small orders.
- Control your costs.
- Produce just-in-time.

cad apparel software

CAD apparel software specifically offers the designer a complete fashion design software solution. It gives the designer the tools and techniques to digitally create designs from the initial concept to final presentation. This includes:

- Rough sketches to Fashion illustrations
- Minibodies, croquis and line drawings for presentations/storyboards
- Color and fashion trends
- Colorways and fabric draping
- Textile design, fabric swatches, universal and seasonal color palettes
- Trim libraries
- Photographic Image Editing
- Individual portfolios

The CAD packages include software to:
- Graphically display menus to easily navigate through files and libraries.
- Create prints, knits and wovens from libraries and from scratch.
- Simulate and design fabrics - wovens, prints, Jacquards, knits; these designs can be taken from a library of designs within the software package and edited as required.
- Use the integrated programs to create your designs, e.g. Easy Knit, Easy Weave, Easy Coloring, Easy Jacquard.
- Design in repeat - any number of repeats can be made using different sequences and sizes.
- Create and manage colorways and color matches for textile designs, fabric swatches, universal and seasonal palettes (to create and manage consistent color values and color matches).
- Create coordinates and colorways and design simple yarn-dyed wovens.
- Create tonal and watercolor prints, sophisticated wovens and jacquards and simulate knits.
- Create 3D Texture Mapping and Draping tools to apply print, woven or knit texture to line drawn sketches or photos of the model/figure. This gives an impression of fabric drape and a more realistic appearance to the design.

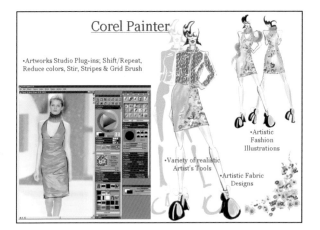

*Imagery courtesy of **Gerber (Artworks)***

- Sketch fashion roughs, illustrations, working drawings and specification drawings

- Integrate scans into the system to be used in the creation of designs and presentations.

- Use libraries of designs and style details - ready made libraries contain fashion figure bodies, individual apparel pieces such as bodices, belts, cuffs, collars, fastenings, closures, pockets etc., which can be updated to create the latest trends for the season for womenswear, menswear and childrenswear.

- Integrate images from other graphic software, e.g. CorelPainter and Photoshop, or use TIF, EPS and JPG files.

- Utilise and manage apparel databases, which include garment-related specifications including fabric, measurements, trims and costing, and importing and exporting elements.

- Create presentations/storyboards, catalogues and portfolio material, which can include croquis, flat sketches, images of the actual model wearing the design, fabrics (prints, weaves, knits) and colorways, etc.

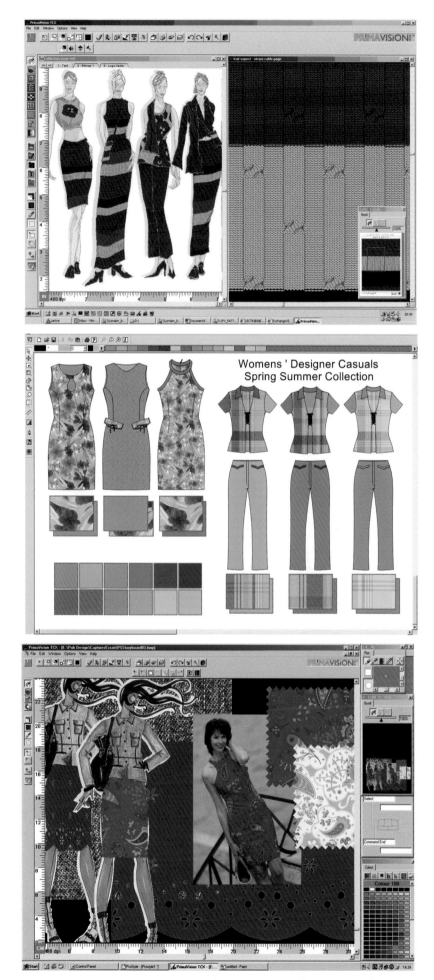

*An **instructor's manual** with exercises will be available for lecturers, see www. knowledgezone.net*

*Imagery courtesy of **Lectra Pty Ltd**, NZ*

appendix **2**
fashion internet

'Cyber slink along classy catwalks' by travelling on the Internet global information highway. The Internet is an excellent tool for researching the latest fashions and trends - from fashion catwalk to street, from stage to screen, from art to music, and all this in less time than it takes to pack a suit case and jump on a plane. Do a **key word** search using a search engine such as Google.

The Internet is your international fashion **Yellow Pages**, an A to Z for accessories, for clothing, fabric and trends; fashion designers and their catwalk shows, trend services, trade shows, fashion associations, retail organizations, PR agencies, stylists, and wholesalers etc. all dedicated to fashion.

Many designers and illustrators have a presence on the Internet with their own web site by presenting their design portfolios and clothing ranges, or simply displaying electronic advertisements for electronic window-shopping. Check out the big names such as Chanel, Lanvin, Giorgio Armani, Paul Smith, Dolce and Gabbana. Numerous fashion magazines are also on-line, for example: Vogue, Elle, and Marie Claire (see *Further Reading*).

Fashion Design Presentation Series created by **Frances Howie,** *Fashion Designer, Lanvin, Paris*

fashion sites

www.apparelnews.net: Trade shows and more.

www.cottoninc.com: Great info - research and promotion company for cotton.

www.fashion.net: Great research site, hypertext links short cuts to other sites, fashion magazines and general industry news.

www.fashionangel.com/angel: Fashion designers and magazines on the Net - updated daily, linked with FUK.

www.fashionguide.com: News, gossip from the entertainment world and serious reports from some of the leading names in fashion journalism.

www.fashionmall.com: An international fashion industry Yellow Pages list from A to Z, dedicated to fashion; update on collections, seasonal highlights and what to wear.

www.fashionplanet.com: Virtual fashion windows of New York; Madison and 5th Avenues etc. with weekly updates.

www.fashionwindows.com: Great site, listing fashion trends, runway shows and a calendar of events.

www.fuk.co.uk: Excellent site with fashion news, shows, art, shopping and what is being worn on the streets in Britain.

www.global-color.com: Forecasting company, information and inspiration for colors and trends.

www.infomat.com: Excellent information on services used by the fashion industry worldwide; from designers, publications to retail organisations.

www.londonfashionweek.co.uk: Great catwalk shows.

www.modaitalia.com: Fashion from Italy plus a lot more such as; textiles, beauty, fashion calendar.

www.promostyl.com: International design agency researching trends, selling their books and products online.

www.thetrendreport.com: Cool site! Fashion runways, editorial and consumer buying.

www.style.com: Excellent site linked with Vogue and W; video and slide coverage of the latest designer fashion shows; celebrity style, trend reports and breaking fashion news.

www.wgsn.com: WGSN, Worth Global Style Network, latest news and reviews of the developing fashions and trends around the world, and daily fashion news.

www.widemedia.com/fashionuk: Great graphics and fashion photography, features articles, profiles, trivia and giveaways.

computer sites

Search on subjects such as Photoshop, scanning, digital cameras, and find sites to help you with technical problems such as; **www.adobe.com** and **www. microsoft.com**

New Sites: This is a constantly developing area as more companies make the transition to using and establishing their presence on the Internet. Key word searches are the only sure way of accessing the latest sites.

further reading

The following list is a selection of books and periodicals, both hard copy and virtual, that will keep you informed about the latest fashion, designers, trends and computing tips. With the growing interest in both fashion and computing, there is an enormous amount of information to be found online. For more information, do a keyword search and visit websites such as R.D. Franks Bookshop, London, <www.rdfranks.co.uk>.

fashion design and illustration

Borrelli, Laird, *Fashion Illustration Now,* T&H
Borrelli, Laird, *Fashion Illustration Next,* T& H
Braddock, S., Techno Textiles: *Revolutionary Fabrics for Fashion and Design,* T&H
Burke, Sandra, *Fashion Artist - Drawing Techniques to Portfolio Presentation,* Burke Publishing
Dawber, Martin, *Imagemakers,* Mitchell Beazley
Jenkyn Jones, Sue, *Fashion Design,* Laurence King
McKelvey, Kathryn, *Fashion Source Book,* Blackwell Science
Ramos, Juan, *Antonio 60, 70, 80: Three Decades of Fashion Illustration,* Thames & Hudson
Stipelman, Steven, *Illustrating Fashion, Concept to Creation,* Fairchild
Tain, Linda, *Portfolio Presentation For Fashion Designers,* Fairchild

fashion computing

Aldrich, Winifred, *CAD in Clothing and Textiles,* Blackwell Science
Chase, Reneé Weiss, *CAD for Fashion Design*
Colussy, M.Kathleen, *Fashion Design on Computers,* Prentice Hall
Gray, Stephen, *CAD/CAM in clothing and Textiles,* Gower Publishing
Miller, Phyllis Bell, *AutoCAD for the Apparel Industry*
Sultan, Barbara, *Computer-Aided Flat Sketching for the Fashion Industry,* Da'Max
Taylor, P., *Computers in the Fashion Industry,* Heinemann
Wesen, Michele Bryant, and, DeMers, Diane, *The Spec Manual,* Fairchild

graphics and general computing

Copestake, Stephen, *PowerPoint 2003,* In easy steps
Haynes, Barry and **Crumpler,** Wendy, *Photoshop Artistry, A Master Class for Photographers and Artists,* SYBEX, Inc.
Meehan, Tim, *Great Photoshop Techniques,* MIS: Press, a subsidiary of Henry Holt and Company, Inc.
Rich, Jim and **Bozek,** Sandy, *Photoshop in Black and White,* Peachpit Press, Inc.
Shufflebotham, Robert, *Photoshop CS,* In easy steps
Shufflebotham, Robert, *InDesign,* In easy steps
Vandome, Nick, *Dreamweaver MX 2004,* In easy steps
Vandome, Nick, *Fireworks MX,* In easy steps
Woolridge, Mike, *Adobe Photoshop 7, Teach Yourself Visually,* Wiley Publishing
Yarnold, Stuart, *Windows XP Tips and Tricks,* In easy steps

management

Burke, Rory, *Project Management Planning and Control Techniques,* Burke Publishing
Burke, Rory, *Small Business Entrepreneur,* Burke Publishing
Burke, Rory, *Small Business Management,* Burke Publishing

periodicals

Another Magazine (British)
Collezioni (Italian): Trends, Sport and Street, Ready to Wear, Accessori, Bambini (children), Donna, Uomo (men)
Dazed and Confused (British)
Depeche Mode (French)
Donna (Italian)
Elle (American, Australian, British, French, German, Italian, SA, Spanish publications)
Fashion Collections GAP (American)
Fashion Show (American)
GQ (men)

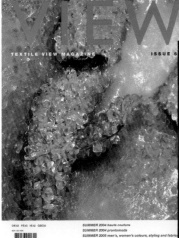

online magazines

Use search engines to look for online fashion magazines: Elle, Harpers Bazaar, Vogue, Marie Claire, Tatler, Lumiere, Women's Wear Daily etc.

www.elle.com: Excellent street style.

www.papermag: New York based magazine focusing on downtown New York, updated daily with cutting edge coverage on fashion, catwalk shows, trends.

www.vogue.com: Vogue guide to European shows and more.

Harpers and Queen (British)

Harper's Bazaar (American, Italian)

ID (British)

Joyce (Hong Kong)

L'Officiel da la Couture (French)

Marie Claire (American, Australian, British, French, German, Italian, SA, Spanish publications)

Oyster (Australian)

Pop (British)

Spruce (British)

The Face (British)

Vogue (American, Australian, British, French, German, Italian, SA, Spanish publications): also **L'Uomo**, Bambini, Vogue Sposa Italia

Wallpaper (British)

techno publications

There are numerous computer magazines, which, although aimed at technology geeks, also have useful snippets of information for the novice.

3D World – features 3D and visual effects

PC Plus

PC Answers

Digital Camera Magazine

Digital Photography Techniques

Computer Arts – excellent for tutorials and creativity using all the popular software such as Photoshop, Illustrator, Flash, Dreamweaver etc.

MACFORMAT – reviews and tutorials for Mac

trade publications

Drapers Record (British)

Fashion Forecast International (British)

Fashion Quarterly (British)

Fashion Theory: The Journal of Body, Dress and Culture (British)

International Textiles (British)

Trends View on Color (British)

View - Textile View Magazine (British)

W (American)

Woman's Wear Daily (WWD) (American)

trend/fashion forecast services

Doneger Design Direction (American)

Faces (British)

Fashion News (British)

Here & There (American)

Jill Lawrence Design (JLD. INTL) (British, fashion and colour)

Lutz Keller (colour)

Nelly Rodi (French, colour and global lifestyles)

Nigel French (American)

Pat Tunsky, Inc. (American)

Promostyl USA (American)

Pro-Specs (forecast software)

Stylists Information Services (SIS) (American)

The Fashion Service (American)

The Wool Bureau (American)

Trend Union (American)

Trends West (American, trends and textiles)

WGSN (Worth Global Style Network) - www.wgsn.com

glossary

Anchor point : Square points that display when an object is selected. The shape of the object can be changed by dragging one or more of its points.

Artboard: The area where the fashion drawing is created and edited.

Bitmap: An image composed of grids of pixels or dots. (See Vector.)

CAD/CAM (Computer Aided Design/Computer Aided Manufacturing): An interactive computer design system for the apparel and textile industry.

Clothing Range/Collection: A number of garments that mix and match and complement each other; designed for a specific season or area of the apparel/fashion industry.

CMYK: A color mode made up of cyan (C), magenta (M), yellow (Y), and black (K). Used for commercial printing of books, periodicals, brochures etc.

Image (Color) Mode: Used to described the make up of an image; black-and-white, grayscale, RGB, CMYK.

Colorway (Color Palette, Color Story): A selection of colors for a collection/range of garments or fabric designs which offers color choices.

Concept/Mood/Theme Board: Creative ideas and designs presented together to show the overall concept or direction for a fashion or fabric collection.

Croquis: A french word to describe a small rough sketch of the figure from which a garment or a clothing range is developed; a line drawing to illustrate a garment or painted design of a fabric.

Croquis (Female/Male Figure Template): A line drawing of the figure with normal body proportions, to be used as a guide for drawing flats/working drawings.

Design Presentations (Storyboards): A fashion designers' creative format to communicate clothing designs and concepts to the design team, buyers, merchandisers, and marketing teams.

Drawing Software: Powerful graphics drawing programs, Illustrator, CorelDRAW, Freehand, for drawing lines and shapes to create flats/working drawings and technical drawings for specs, fashion illustrations and presentation work.

EPS (Encapsulated PostScript): The best file format for vector images; supported by most graphics software (will only print the 'preview' on non postscript printers e.g. inkjets).

Fabric Swatch: A small sample of fabric to indicate color, fabric quality, texture and print which can be presented as part of design presentations, mood boards etc.

Fashion Designers: Design and sketch garments to communicate fashion designs and concepts to a design team, pattern makers, sample machinists, and buyers. They are required to draw well to make their designs understood, but they do not necessarily need to excel in the more stylised art of fashion illustration.

Fashion Illustrations: Sketches of the clothed figure that aim to achieve an impression of a design. Fashion illustration is a commercial art form in its own right, a way to express and accentuate a fashion design to present to a client. Artistic license is normal practise, for example, the fashion figure may be longer in the legs for a more stylish and dramatic impact.

Fashion Illustrators: Give a signature style to a fashion designer's creation. Using creative drawing skills, an illustrator builds on and enhances the fashion designer's fashion sketches.

Fashion and Fabric Shows/Exhibitions: Globally, fashion and textile trade events are held throughout the year and tend to focus on the seasons, Spring/Summer and Autumn/Winter. Textile fairs are held a year ahead of the manufactured clothes reaching the stores; this allows sufficient lead time for designers to sample the fabrics for their collections. Fashion trade fairs and catwalk shows have a six months lead time before the clothing hits the stores. These shows are a central point for exhibitors, buyers, designers and the press to come together and do business - buying and selling merchandise, or forecasting and reporting future trends.

Fill: A color, bitmap, gradient (fountain), or pattern applied to an area of an image.

Flats (Working Drawings/Diagrammatics): Explicit line drawings of garments, drawn to scale, using simple, clear lines, with no exaggeration of detail as you would find in a more stylized fashion illustration. All construction lines such as seams, darts, and styling details, such as pockets, buttons, and trims, are represented.

GIF (Graphics Interchange Format): A graphics file format which uses compression creating a small file size, therefore, excellent for the Internet; commonly used for images with solid blocks of color such as logos and lettering.

Gradient (Fountain Fill): A smooth progression of two or more colors applied to an area of an image; the gradient may take on a linear, radial, conical, or square appearance.

Grayscale: A color mode that displays images using 256 shades of gray.

Grid: A series of evenly spaced horizontal and vertical dots that are used to help precision when drawing and arranging objects.

Group: A set of objects that behave as one.

Guideline: A horizontal, vertical, or slanted line that can be placed anywhere in the drawing window to aid the placement of objects.

Handles: A set of eight squares that appear at the corners and sides of an object when the object is selected. By dragging individual handles, you can scale, resize or mirror the object. If you click a selected object, the shape of the handles changes to arrows so that you can transform the object, rotate and skew etc.

Icon: A small pictorial representation of a tool, object or file.

Image Editing Software: Photoshop, industry standard software for image editing, is a powerful paint and photo editing program - import, edit and manipulate scanned/digital images, or create images from the initial concept. Images created in drawing packages can be brought into Photoshop to create impressive fashion and fabric presentations for printing and the Web.

Drop Shadow: A three-dimensional shadow effect that gives objects the appearance of depth.

Insert (Import/Place): The command/technique used to bring an image, object or clipart into a drawing.

JPEG (Joint Photographic Experts Group): Use this file format for the Web and email attachments; creates a very small file size by compression (keep a master copy as JPEG compression causes quality losses each time it is saved). (Unsuitable for images with solid blocks of color e.g. line drawings).

Layers: Typically, you work in multiple layers when using graphics software. Layers allow you to keep elements in the image separate so that each layer can be edited individually. This is especially useful when working with complex images with many elements e.g. a fashion design presentation.

Library of Styles: Fashion libraries are excellent for retrieving files such as dress shapes, skirt shapes, various collars, cuffs etc. Digital libraries are particularly important for fashion designers because, as their portfolio of digital designs develops they will spend less time drawing from scratch and more time manipulating and adapting existing designs.

Mannequin: A dress form, modelled on the human body, with style lines that correspond to the fit and construction lines from which clothing patterns and garments are made.

Menu Bar: Displays Menu Commands - choose a command on the menu bar to display a dropdown list e.g. Choose View (Menu Bar)>Guides>Lock Guides.

Object: A generic term for any item you create or place in a drawing. Objects include lines, shapes, graphics, and text.

Palettes: Display editing and monitoring options e.g. color (RGB, CMYK), swatches, brushes, stroke weight (line thickness), dashed lines, gradient, transparency, layers, align. To select a palette choose Window (Menu Bar). These small windows can be moved around the Work Area.

Paths: The basic component from which objects are constructed. For example, as you click and draw with the Pen Tool, anchor points are formed producing a 'path'. A 'path' can be 'open' (a line or shape with end points unconnected), or 'closed' (a circle or shape with ends connected).

Pattern Fill: A fill consisting of a series of repeating vector objects or images.

PDF: Use this file format for the Web, email attachments and commercial printing. Read files using Acrobat Reader (free download). This means that you do not need the original program to read the file.

Pixel: A colored dot that is the smallest part of a bitmap. (See Resolution.)

PowerPoint: Creates presentations for screen (slide show/video/web/email attachments).

Presentation: (Boards, portfolio, fashion presentation, design presentation), the professional method used to visually display a design concept in a creative, dynamic format, enhancing individual pieces of artwork. The concept could be for a fashion range, a fashion mood or theme, fashion colours, fashion fabrics or fashion promotion. Individually, sketches can look flat and uninteresting, but if all the right ingredients are grouped together in a well planned layout, the theme will be strong and commercially successful. Designers and illustrators use many presentation techniques to enhance their artwork.

PSD (Photoshop - Native Image Format): Retains layers - this is the best format if you still need to make changes to your individual and composite images.

Rasterized Image: An image that has been rendered into pixels - the image can then be edited in an image editing program. When you convert vector graphics files to bitmap files, you create rasterized images.

Resolution: The number of pixels per inch in a bitmap measured in ppi (pixels per inch) or dpi (dots per inch). Low resolutions can result in a grainy appearance to the bitmap; high resolutions can produce smoother images but result in larger file sizes. Low resolutions, 72 dpi, are used for images for the Internet, high resolutions of 300 dpi are used for commercial printing.

RGB (Red, Green, Blue): The most common mode for working with color images - photographs, fashion drawings and illustrations for general printing and web/screen. RGB is faster to work with than CMYK, as it creates a smaller file size (for this reason, if your image is for commercial printing, convert to CMYK once all changes have been made to the image).

Roughs: These are quick drawings capturing ideas and concepts in a sketch book, and usually drawn using a pencil, fine liner or marker pen.

Rotate: To reposition and reorient an object by turning it around its center of rotation.

Rulers and Guides: Horizontal and vertical rulers and guides are used to enable precise positioning and alignment of elements e.g. positioning the centre front line to an exact point. Rulers and guides are non-printing and can be displayed or hidden.

Sample Garment (Toile, Muslin): A trial garment made from a pattern which has been interpreted from a designer's sketch. Initially made from an inferior fabric such as calico.

Sketch Book: (Fashion journal, fashion diary, work book and croquis sketch book), drawing pad used to sketch innovative ideas for designs, and collate images, color and fabric swatches. Sketch books are your visual reference data base and a valuable source of information for your design projects.

Skew: To slant an object vertically, horizontally, or both.

Snap: With 'Snap' selected (active) an object that is being drawn or moved will align automatically to a point on the grid, a guideline, or another object.

Specs (Specification sheet): A 'spec' sheet is a document that contains an accurately drawn flat, and specifications (instructions and measurements). This information is needed to produce garments to the required standard and design. It forms the basis of a binding contract between the design house or client, and the factory that produces the garment. With a large percentage of clothing manufacturing being outsourced offshore, this document must be clear, precise and self explanatory.

Street Fashion: The fashion and clothing that the public are wearing and the innovative way they put it together.

Style Lines: The fit, shape and construction details that make up a garment.

Stylised: A drawing that is non-realistic and has a signature look about it that identifies it with the artist.

Swatch (Color Swatch in Computing Software): One of a series of solid-colored patches used as a sample when selecting color. Swatch also refers to the colors contained in the color palette. (See Fabric Swatch.)

Status Bar: Displays information about the open document and the tool currently being used.

Storyboards: (See Presentations).

Technical Drawings: (See Flats, and Specs).

Template: (See Croquis).

TIFF (Tagged Image Format): Universal graphics format supported by most graphics software, word processing, page layout software - supports layers but images are best flattened to create a smaller file size.

Toolbox: Displays the drawing and editing tools as icons. Click on a tool to select it - a small triangle next to the tool icon indicates hidden tools - click on the triangle to open and select another tool. These hidden tools can be torn off/floated and moved around the work area - a useful feature for frequently used tools.

Vector: An image/object created by a mathematical formula which forms smooth lines and curves which are 'resolution independent' and, therefore, can be scaled up or down without deterioration, and remain sharp and clear.

Work Area (Workspace): The starting point for all drawing packages is the Work Area. The drawing tools and commands are selected from the *Tool Box, Menu Bar* and the *Palettes* which appear within the Work Area.

Working Drawing: (See Flats, and Specs).

Zoom (Zoom In, Zoom Out): To reduce or magnify the view of a drawing. You can zoom in to see details or zoom out for a broader view.

ZIP (Stuffit (Mac), Winzip (PC)): A lossless file compression technique that results in smaller file size and faster processing time. Excellent for sending files using the Internet.

index

10 key fashion image editing techniques, (Photoshop), 92-105

20 key fashion drawing techniques (drawing exercises), 32-43

AI (.ai) (Adobe Illustrator extension), 24
anchor points (nodes), 35
- deleting, (nodes), 35
- selecting (nodes), 34
Apple (see Mac), 15, 25
art box, 17
artboard, 28
Austin, Naomi, 9

Background color, 108
bitmap
- images, 20, 22
- mode, 22
blouses, (women), 83
bodysuits (children), 81
books by burke publishing, 174-176
Bradford College, 11, 12
Brush Tool, 113
Bureaux Design, 17, 136, 137, 153

CAD apparel software, 160
CAD, 156-161
CAD/CAM, 11
canvas size, change, 95
CDR (.cdr) (CorelDraw extension), 24
change the canvas size, 95
channels, 23
Chelsea West, 92, 97, 102, 110, 111, 112, 120, 123, 130, 131
childrenswear presentation, 78
childrenswear, 78-83
circles, drawing, 37
CMYK, 22
color
- filling objects, flats, 41
- paint and draw, 113,
- effects, 106-121
- overlay on a flat, 120

Color Picker Palette, 108
Color Range Command, 100
computer
- basics, 19
- toolkit, 14-17
- training, 19
Cook, Lynnette, 10, 12, 26, 43, 53, 78, 79, 82, 83, 150, 151
copy and paste
- scanned fashion illustration, 103
- selection, 102
CorelDRAW
- tools, 27–43
- Toolbox, 30
create
- figure template (croquis), 46
- new file, 92
- new image, 32
- type, 118-119
creating presentations, 125
creating text/type 38, 118-119
crop an image, 92
croquis
- female (figure template), 46, 47
- male (figure template), 73
Davies, Christopher, 12, 21, 22, 100, 117, 123, 134, 135, 146, 147
Davies, Louise, 3, 9
Define a Pattern, 112
deleting anchor points (nodes), 35
design
- details, 66-67
- portfolio, 153
- presentation exercises, 126-135
- presentations, 70, 78, 123, 125, 136-151
Dewhirst Group, 15
digital
- design portfolio, 152-155
- photography, 84-87
- portfolio, 152-155

digitised images, 87

draped look, garment, Filter, 116

drawing

- circles and ovals, 37

- flats, women, 27-43, 44-71

- flats, men, 72-77

- flats, children, 79-83

- lines (strokes), 33

- rectangles (pockets) 37

- techniques, 26-43

- dresses (women), 64-65

- dresses (children), 82

Drop Shadow, 119

dungarees, (babies), 80

Duotone, 22

DVD, 25

Edit

- command, 95

- Type, 38, 118-119

Elliptical Marquee Tool, 97

EPS (.eps) (Encapsulated PostScript), 24, 43

erase elements/pixels, 114

erase, 114

Eyedropper Tool, 108

Farmer, Jonathan Kyle, 148, 149

fashion

- computing tool kit, 14-17

- illustration, copy and paste to another image, 103

- illustration, sharpen, 115

- industry drawing software, 27

- Internet, 162-163

- sites, 163

- umbrella, (fashion), 12

female croquis (figure template), 46

FH (.fh) (Freehand extension), 24

file

- formats, 24

- management, 19

- saving, 24, 71, 87, 124, 155

Fill

- background of a flat with a Gradient, 111

- fashion illustration with color, 110

- flat with a Pattern, 112

- flat with color, 110

- flats/objects with a gradient, 42

- objects (flats), 41

- selection with a color, 110

- selection with a Gradient, 111

- selection with a Pattern, 112

- type with a Gradient, 119

- type with a Pattern, 119

Filters, 115-119

fitted

- dress, 64

- pant, 61

- shirt, 52

- skirt (pencil), 56

flats

- and specs women, 44-56

- children, 79-83

- men, 72-77

- women, 44-71, 130-131, 134-137, 153

- working drawings, 12, 17

flatten, 23

Foreground color, 108

Foschini, 92, 101, 108, 115, 125

Freehand

- Toolbox, 30

- tools, 27- 43

gallery of design presentations, 136-151

Gerber (Gerber Technology), 157, 160

GIF (.gif), 24

glossary, 166

Gradient

- fill, 111

- filling flats/objects, 42

- type 119

graphics drawing packages, 15

Grayscale, 22

guides (and rulers), 32

hard drives (portable), 25

history

- computing 11

- palette, 95

hot tips (presentations), 124

Howie, Frances, 46, 84, 97, 110, 114, 123, 132, 133, 142, 143, 144, 145, 146, 162, 164

Illustrator

- Toolbox, 29

- tools, 27- 43

- work area, 28

Image editing program, 15

image modes (RGB, CMYK, grayscale, duotone, bitmap mode), 22

jacket
- childrens, 81
- mens, 74-75
- women, 69

Joseph, Kim, 98

JPEG (.jpeg) (Joint Photographic Experts Group), 24

Kaur, Kashmir, 12

Keshav, Yatika, 14

kids bodysuits and jackets, 81

kids swims, 80

Lasso Tool, 97

Layer Styles, 120

layers, 23, 24, 104

Learmont, Bindi, 116

Lectra Cad Suite, 157, 158

Lectra Pty Ltd, (SnapFashun), 71, 80, 81, 82, 83, 156, 157, 158, 159, 161

library of styles, 71

Live Trace (Illustrator), 43

Logan, Linda, 53, 55, 59, 62, 63, 65, 66

Mac (see Apple), 15, 25

Magic Wand Tool, 99

Magnetic Lasso Tool, 98

male croquis (figure template), 73

marching ants, 96

Marquee Tools, 96, 99

McKenzie, Stuart, 12, 19, 44, 87, 88, 93, 95, 106, 108, 124, 125, 140, 141, 153, 154, 155

memory sticks, 25

menswear, 72-77

Microsoft Office, 15

mirroring (reflecting) object (flats), 40

move
- selection, 101
- around an image, 93

native file format, 24, 43

new image, 32

Ng, Michael, 12, 21, 22, 117, 123, 134, 135

node
- anchor points, 35
- deleting, (anchor points), 35
- selecting (anchor points), 34

O'Dea, Rory, 18

opacity,
- photograph on a layer, 105
- Type, 119

open an image, 92

ovals, drawing, 37

Paint
- draw with color, 113
- Brush Tool, 113

palettes, 28

pants
- childrens, 78, 82
- mens, 77

women, 61-63

Path, close, open, 113

Pattern, type 119

PC, 15

PDF (.pdf), 24

Pencil Tool, 113

photograph, 84-87
- sharpen, 115

Photoshop
- color and effects, 106-121

essential tools, 88-105
- exercises, 92-104, 108-121
- toolbox, 91

pixels, erase, 114

pockets
- design details, 66-67
- drawing, 37
- scaling, 39

Polygonal Lasso Tool, 98

portable hard drives, 25

PowerPoint presentation, 154

PowerTRACE (CorelDRAW), 43

presentation, 70, 78, 123, 125, 136-151

printing color, 25

PSD (.psd), 24

Pumpkin Patch, 78

rasterize, Type, 119

Rectangle Marquee Tool, 96

rectangles, drawing, 37

redo, 95

reflecting, 40, 49-52, 56, 60, 64, 74

removable media, 25

resolution, 21, 86

return an image to a previous state, 95

revert, 95

RGB, 22

rompers (babies), 80

rotate an image, 92

rotating objects, 38

rulers and guides, 32

saving files, 24, 71, 87, 124, 155

scaling an object (pocket), 39

scanning and digital photography, 84-87

scanning tips, 85-86

select Foreground and Background Colors, 108

selecting

- anchor points (nodes), 34

- objects (flats), 34

selection

- move, 101

- copy and paste, 102

sending objects (flats) to the front or back, 41

shaping

- flats, 36

- lines (objects), 36

Sharpen

- scanned fashion illustration, 115

- scanned photograph, 115

shirts

- children, 83

- mens, 76

- women, 52, 54-55

shortcut tips, 121

Simmonds, Esther, 3

single breasted jacket (mens), 74

skirts

- children, 79, 82

- women, 56-59

specs (specification sheets), 68

status bar, 28

Stoddart, Susan, 11

Stroke

- fabric swatch, 114

- fashion illustration, 114

- selection, 114

Stytsenko-Berdnik, Alissa, 13, 72, 85, 99, 103, 104, 105, 121, 122, 123, 126, 127, 138, 139, 152

Swatches palette, 109

swims (kids), 80

table (exercises)

- childrenswear flats, 78

- presentations (design), 123

- drawing techniques, 27

- flats, women, 45

- menswear, 73

- Photoshop essential tools, 89

- Photoshop, color and effects, 107

table of software, 16

tank top (stretch fabric), 48

terminology, 31

text, (type), 38, 118-119

TIFF (Tagged Image Format), 43

tips, shortcut, 121, 124

Toolbox, 28

- CorelDRAW, 30

- Freehand, 30

- Illustrator, 29

- Photoshop, 91

tools (Illustrator, CorelDRAW, Freehand), 27– 43

top with sleeves (stretch fabric), 50

tops

- childrens, 78-79, 82-83

- mens, 76

- women, 48-51, 53, 55

tracing [pen tool, Live Trace (Illustrator), Corel PowerTRACE (CorelDRAW) and tracing software], 43

training (computer), 19

type in a bounding box, 118

type, text, 38, 118-119

vector images, 20, 24

view and move around an image, 93

web, 16, 24

Windows (PC), 15, 25

Windows and Mac, 25

work area

- Illustrator, 27, 28

- Photoshop, 90

working drawings, see flats, and specs

World, 9, 12, 21, 22, 117, 123, 134, 135, 147

zoom in/out, 39, 93, 121

project management series

The *Project Management Series* promotes Entrepreneurship and Project Management tools and techniques. In our competitive world the successful manager needs entrepreneurship skills to spot opportunities, and project management skills to make-it-happen.

Introduction to Project Management
Rory Burke
ISBN: 0-9582 733-3-2, 288 pages

This book is a broad based introduction to the field of Project Management which explains all the special planning and control techniques needed to manage projects successfully. This book is ideal for managers entering project management and team members in the project management office (PMO).

Project Management - Planning and Control Techniques (5ed)
Rory Burke
ISBN 0-9582 733-1-6, 384 pages

PM 5ed presents the latest planning and control techniques, particularly those used by the project management software and the body of knowledge (APM bok and PMI's PMBOK). This book has established itself internationally as the standard text for Project Management programs.

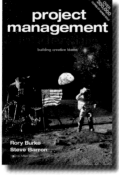

Project Management Leadership - Building Creative Teams
Rory Burke and Steve Baron
ISBN 0-9582 733-5-9, 384 pages

This book is a comprehensive guide outlining the essential leadership skills to manage the human side of managing projects. Key topics include: leadership styles, delegation, motivation, negotiation, conflict resolution, and team building.

Entrepreneurs Toolkit
Rory Burke
ISBN: 0-9582 391-4-2, 160 pages

Entrepreneurs Toolkit is a comprehensive guide outlining the essential entrepreneur skills to spot a marketable opportunity, the essential business skills to start a new venture and the essential management skills to make-it-happen.

Small Business Entrepreneur
Rory Burke
ISBN: 0-9582 391-6-9, 160 pages

Small Business Entrepreneur is a comprehensive guide outlining the essential management skills to run a small business on a day-to-day basis. This includes developing a business plan and sources of finance.

www.burkepublishing.com